'John's experience and wisdom sings out in the book, it's like he is in the room with you. The book provides structure, focus and positive encouragement for anyone looking for a new job.'

Rosemary McLean, International Career Strategist, Career Innovation

'Insightful, well thought out and inspirational, *Just The Job!* takes a systematic approach to job hunting – giving you the confidence you need to get the job you always dreamed of.'

Rachel Burge, Director, Content Creatives, freelance writer for Career Builder

'If you believe there are no good jobs out there, if you can't face sending out another CV, or if you are tired of spending hours on your computer searching out opportunities, this book is the arm around your shoulder you need. For the jaded job searcher this book is an injection of fresh thinking to equip you to get the job you deserve.'

Carole Pemberton, career coach, author and Visiting Professor, Ulster University

'When I read John's writing, two things happen. First, I feel as if he's standing right there, personally advising me. And second, I always come away thinking over the issue in a new way. It's a rare, but very useful, gift.'

Sarah Green, Associate Editor, *Harvard Business Review*

'For years, John Lees has been the smartest voice in career coaching. His insight and advice are a must-read for anyone entering today's competitive job market.'

Rebecca Alexander, Dossier Editor, *Psychologies Magazine*

'John Lees' approach works, because he gives readers simple, practical steps to help flip their mindsets into the more daring, exploratory and confident mode needed for career transition success.'

Stuart Lindenfield, Head of Transitions Practice, Reed Consulting

'John Lees' writing offers insight and knowledge which allows you to think in new ways and achieve changes you didn't think possible. In these difficult and challenging times, his books help you achieve your next career step.'

Laura Roberts, Chief Executive, NHS Manchester

'John Lees is the career professional's professional; the doyen of careers experts. His books and advice have helped countless numbers of people to enjoy better, more fulfilling careers.'

Dr Harry Freedman, Career and Business Strategist, Hanover Executive

Just the Job!

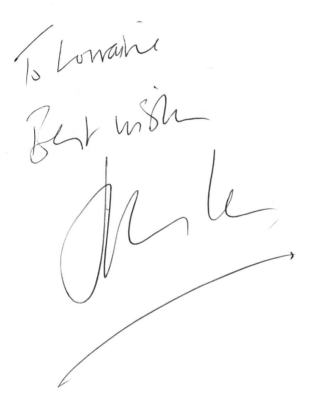

To Lorraine

Best wishes

Just the Job!

Smart and fast strategies
to get the perfect job

JOHN LEES

Harlow, England • London • New York • Boston • San Francisco • Toronto • Sydney • Auckland • Singapore • Hong Kong
Tokyo • Seoul • Taipei • New Delhi • Cape Town • São Paulo • Mexico City • Madrid • Amsterdam • Munich • Paris • Milan

PEARSON EDUCATION LIMITED

Edinburgh Gate
Harlow CM20 2JE
United Kingdom
Tel: +44 (0)1279 623623
Fax: +44 (0)1279 431059
Web: www.pearson.com/uk

First published 2013 (print and electronic)

© John Lees 2013 (print and electronic)

The right of John Lees to be identified as author of this work has been asserted by him in accordance with the Copyright, Designs and Patents Act 1988.

Pearson Education is not responsible for the content of third-party internet sites.

ISBN: 978-0-273-77246-0 (print)
        978-0-273-77247-7 (PDF)
        978-0-273-77248-4 (ePub)

British Library Cataloguing-in-Publication Data
A catalogue record for the print edition is available from the British Library

Library of Congress Cataloging-in-Publication Data
A catalog record for the print edition is available from the Library of Congress

10 9 8 7 6 5 4 3 2
16 15 14

Designed by Design Deluxe
Cover design by Kit Foster

Print edition typeset in 11/14pt Sabon LT Std by 3

Printed in Great Britain by Henry Ling Limited, at the Dorset Press, Dorchester, DT1 1HD

NOTE THAT ANY PAGE CROSS REFERENCES REFER TO THE PRINT EDITION

Contents

About the author

JOHN LEES IS ONE OF the UK's best-known and most trusted career strategists. Through his frequent broadcasts, articles, speaking events and one-to-one consultancy he has helped thousands of people find a fulfilling and happy working life. This expertise has seen John travel from USA to South Africa, Australia and New Zealand to Switzerland, sharing his well honed advice on how to find, keep and progress a top notch career.

As well as writing for major national media such as *The Times, Metro, The Guardian* and *Psychologies* he is also a bestselling author. His book *How To Get A Job You'll Love* regularly tops the bestseller lists and has twice been selected as WH Smith's 'Business Book of the Month'. His other titles include *The Interview Expert* (Pearson), *Take Control of Your Career* and *Job Interviews: Top Answers To Tough Questions* (McGraw-Hill). He broadcasts widely for the BBC, Channel 4 and ITV. He also writes a regular blog for The Harvard Business Review online.

After graduating from the universities of Cambridge, London and Liverpool, John has spent most of his career focusing on the world of work. His clients have included: British Gas Commercial, The British Council, Career Management Consultants Ltd, CIPD, Cranfield School of Management,

The House of Commons, Imperial College, Orange, REC, The Association of MBAs, Lloyds Banking Group, Marks & Spencer, Reuters and Tribal, as well as business schools across the UK. John is a Fellow of the CIPD, an Honorary Fellow of the Institute of Recruitment Professionals, a Career Management Fellow, Joint Chair of ACPi-UK, and the former Chief Executive of the Institute of Employment Consultants. Alongside his careers work John serves as an ordained Anglican priest in the Diocese of Chester. He lives and works in Cheshire, with his wife, the children's writer, Jan Dean, with occasional visits from their two adult sons.

John Lees Associates provides one-to-one career coaching in most parts of the UK. For details plus information about talks and workshops given by John Lees visit www.johnleesca reers.com.

Acknowledgements

WITH AGE COMES, RATHER LATER than it should, a realisation of those many people I haven't thanked enough.

I owe a huge debt to Richard Nelson Bolles, author of the world-famous *What Color Is Your Parachute?* My work as a career strategist was inspired by the creativity, wisdom and generosity of 125 hours' teaching from Dick Bolles at two of his summer workshops in Bend, Oregon, and over a decade of encouragement and support.

Thanks to those who have recently invited me to write about work and careers: James Brockett (People Management), Sarah Green (Harvard Business Review online), Martin Stevens (*Metro*), and to those who have allowed me to road test ideas with different audiences: Judith Armatage, Isabel Chadwick and Robin Wood (Career Management Consultants Ltd), Graeme Dixon and Steve Gorton (AMBA), Suchi Mukherjee (Gumtree), Deborah Hockham (I Am Events), Lorraine Silverman, Janie Wilson (Can Do It Now).

I am enormously grateful to all those who shaped and challenged my thinking about job hunting in the course of writing this book, many of whom appear in its pages as contributors: Gill Best, Jo Bond, Keith Busfield, Julian Childs, Stephanie Clarke, Angella Clarke-Jervoise, Claire Coldwell,

Jane Downes, Zena Everett, Matthias Feist, Peter Fennah, Pauline Godley, Dudley Harrop, Leon Hendra, Kate Howlett, Cathy Kay, Stuart McIntosh, Brian McIvor, Rob Nathan, Al Owens, Daniel Porot, Steve Preston, Robin Rose, Cheryl Roshak, Sophie Rowan, Malcolm Watt, John Whapham, Ruth Winden, and fellow members of the LinkedIn Career Coach Forum.

I owe enormous thanks to my attentive, creative editor at Pearson, Elie Williams. My huge appreciation also goes to my agent James Wills at Watson, Little, for his diligence and encouragement.

This book is dedicated to the memory of Sue Blake (1961–2012), expert publicist and shining friend. I couldn't have got here without you.

PUBLISHER'S ACKNOWLEDGEMENT

We are grateful to *Harvard Business Review Online* for permission to reproduce 'The Lonely Lobby of the Job Hotel', originally published on HBR.org.

OVERVIEW – YOUR JOB HUNTING PLAN

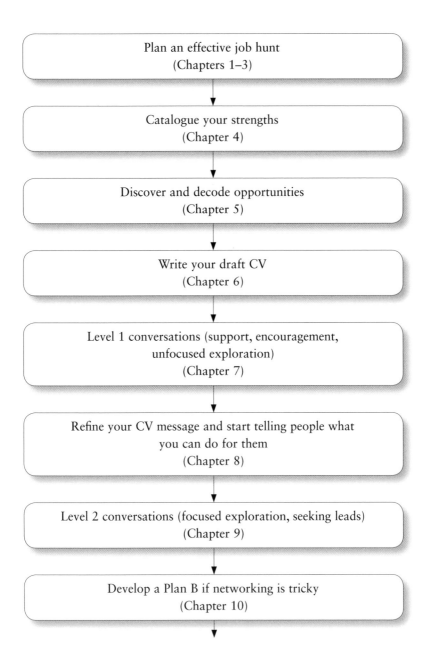

Plan an effective job hunt
(Chapters 1–3)

Catalogue your strengths
(Chapter 4)

Discover and decode opportunities
(Chapter 5)

Write your draft CV
(Chapter 6)

Level 1 conversations (support, encouragement,
unfocused exploration)
(Chapter 7)

Refine your CV message and start telling people what
you can do for them
(Chapter 8)

Level 2 conversations (focused exploration, seeking leads)
(Chapter 9)

Develop a Plan B if networking is tricky
(Chapter 10)

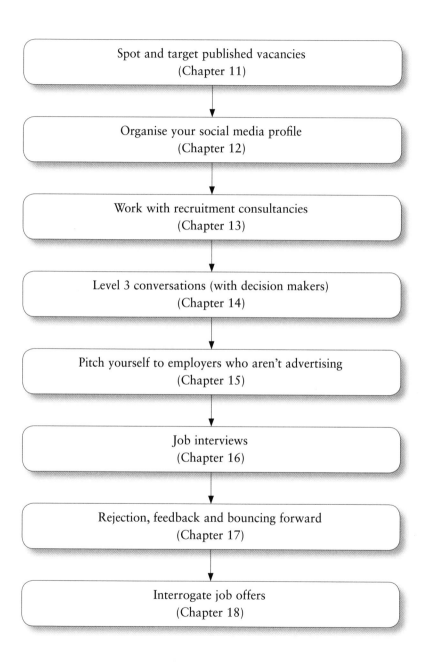

Spot and target published vacancies
(Chapter 11)

Organise your social media profile
(Chapter 12)

Work with recruitment consultancies
(Chapter 13)

Level 3 conversations (with decision makers)
(Chapter 14)

Pitch yourself to employers who aren't advertising
(Chapter 15)

Job interviews
(Chapter 16)

Rejection, feedback and bouncing forward
(Chapter 17)

Interrogate job offers
(Chapter 18)

List of worksheets

IF YOU WOULD LIKE LARGER, A4 versions of these worksheets they can be downloaded free of charge from www.johnleescareers.com/downloads.asp.

Preface – the lonely lobby of the job hotel

I'M LOSING AN ARGUMENT WITH BILL, one of my clients. He's been looking for a job for five months and, like so many at this stage, announces that he is 'lowering his sights' in terms of salary and status. He plays his trump card: 'Listen, John – there are only so many jobs out there. The best job search in the world can't change that fact. Let's be realistic …'

I'm tempted to jump on that last word, because the word *realistic* is too often a second-hand picture of reality. People have been telling me 'this is a really bad year to be looking for a new job' every year for two decades. But I'll take Bill's main point on the chin. If there aren't enough jobs to go around, what's the point of jazzing up your job hunting strategy? Some cynics say that all any job hunt programme does is to distract you with exercises and lists of activity until you drop your hope of a dream job and start fighting for the scraps the market has to offer.

What's really going on here is one big unstated reality. 'Bill,' I say, 'five years ago people fell into jobs. They went to the market with a strategy that was just about working and found jobs that were just about right. Today a lack-lustre job hunt will net you virtually nothing.' Bill is looking glum, so I tell him about the job hotel: 'Three years ago when you were made redundant you visited the job hotel. You stood in the lobby looking vaguely hopeful and people came up to you and offered you things. There were hotel staff around to help. The big, well-signposted conference rooms just off the lobby were full of exhibitions and presentations. The help desks were manned. There were queues of people offering you invitations, wanting to know more about you.

'This week you go back to the job hotel and now the lobby is full of people who have lost their luggage and missed their flights. Everyone is shouting whilst at the same time trying to solve their own problems. The only person available to help is the night porter, who doesn't have very good English and has no idea where the keys are kept. There may be helpful people around, but nothing is signposted and all the doors are locked. So you and several hundred people spend all night knocking timidly on doors that probably won't open, getting no answers, and eventually you end up commiserating with each other in the bar. Yet amidst all the chaos, some people arrive, get what they want and leave. How did they do that?'

The analogy is imperfect, but at least Bill smiles. He's starting to get my point. There are times when the job hotel is kind to the passive traveller – you will be processed and packaged. When a storm comes and the power lines are down, when times are difficult, the hotel is packed with people it can't help. People hang around the lobby, or keep trying doors they know are closed. However, some people do leave the lobby of the job hotel. The customers who get some kind of result are the ones who go off-limits, the ones who go down the road to somewhere else, the ones who organise, improvise and seek hidden solutions, even if that means exploring in broom cupboards or the closed hotel ballroom.

In tough times, 'something will come along' doesn't cut it. It can lead to a distinctly unhealthy cycle of joblessness and discouragement. Today's job hunter is looking for an edge, for a killer CV, for knockout interview answers, but realises that finding a job is also a numbers game requiring long-term stamina. However, identifying a job that is going to be a good fit requires more than perseverance. In a noisy market it's harder for the right employer and candidate to meet. Today's expert job hunter looks at angles, not numbers. What can you do differently to get you closer to the right kinds of conversations?

There *are* roles out there: organisations are looking for enthusiastic and capable people and don't know how to find them. But the mass market doesn't work for candidates or employers – every appointment is a niche appointment. The right jobs are even harder to find. They are unlikely to be advertised. Often what you need is the right conversation at the moment a decision maker has an unsolved problem or an opportunity. It also helps to have the patience not to panic and to keep yourself in the right state of mind to seize opportunities when they arise.

Today's job seeker needs laser-guided applications, not blanket bombing. Undertake your career transition as professionally and openly as if you were doing it for someone else – building on possibilities, staying curious, always asking for connections and ideas, and taking rejection as part of the deal. There's no perfect solution, but it's clear that the process of having conversations with people seems in some way to be at the heart of a better approach, one that shortens job hunting time and gets you a job that feels worth doing at least three days out of five.

(An earlier version of this piece by John Lees was published by Harvard Business Review Online at HBR.org – reprinted here with permission.)

CHAPTER ONE

Your job hunting plan

THIS CHAPTER LOOKS AT:

● Preparing for job hunting in a tough market

● The things that might pass for planning

● Why planning might help more than you think

● An outline of your job hunting campaign

PLANNING FOR AN UPHILL STRUGGLE?

You don't need a book to tell you what it's like looking for a job in a tough market – unemployment levels are rarely out of the news. There are plenty of people competing for jobs, and employers have their pick from a strong field of candidates. Friends and family will almost gleefully tell you about people they know who have been forced to take poorly paid (or unpaid) jobs, or people who have applied for over a thousand jobs without success. We seem to enjoy painting the grimmest possible picture. Every depressing story feels as if it adds more kilos to your rucksack. What seemed like a long but manageable walk on level ground has now become an uphill climb carrying half your body weight. Bad news makes us see difficulty and scarcity rather than glimpses of opportunity.

And yet, interestingly, many people felt exactly the same way about job hunting just a few years back when jobs were abundant. The media still emphasised stories about lay-offs and closures, and even then people felt they had very limited choices. People gave up too soon, limited their options, lowered their sights, when jobs were plentiful. That should tell us all something very important – how you *feel* about job hunting matters. The mindset you adopt is just as important as planning or activity. It is vital not to under-estimate the difficulties of today's marketplace. Yet, even in a recession employers still find it hard to recruit the right people, and some of the people who have the right skills fail to get noticed. The market continues to reveal varied and extensive opportunities to the expert job hunter.

You may feel you have time on your hands when job hunting, but your energy is finite. Many put that energy into worrying about how long they will be out of work rather than into a simple and effective job hunting plan.

WHAT MAKES AN ABOVE AVERAGE JOB HUNTING PERFORMANCE?

This book draws extensively on the views of experts who help people find jobs. Career coach Stuart McIntosh is very aware of the dilemma faced by many job seekers today:

> They have a tendency to fear the worst (end of the world, they're on the scrapheap), they do not see their skills as transferable and opt for a 'better in a job than out of a job' comfort blanket to justify applying for roles well beneath their current skill and pay level, on the basis that they will keep looking for a better job once they are in a job. The problem is that they get stuck in low paid jobs with poor job satisfaction.

Many people rush to the market in this way, worrying about the impact of unemployment on their work history, not realising that, in Stuart McIntosh's terms:

> Employers will accept periods of unemployment as long as

you can demonstrate intelligent job searching, and your 'sell-by-date' can extend for up to 12 months without damage to your brand.

What do top job hunters do differently? You might think they have more marketable skills, have fantastic connections and a brilliant CV. You might believe that they are more aggressive, more energised, happier to knock down doors and push themselves forward. Be careful with that kind of thinking – believing 'I'm not an aggressive job seeker' is a good way of saying 'I can go easy on myself if I don't push as hard as I can'. Look at the **Job Search Preferences** table below. Firstly, consider how often you engage in the activities listed. Reflect honestly on the difference between what you do, and what you talk about doing. Next, look at how comfortable you feel about the activities your job hunting campaign will need to include. Your results will show the gaps in your performance and those areas you will find reasons to avoid.

GETTING A PLAN TOGETHER

Everyone has some kind of job hunting plan, even if it's 'I'll buy an evening paper'. Some planning is constructive – a list of people you need to talk to, perhaps, or plans to attend events and conferences where you might meet useful people. Other plans feel more like the words of the Schultz cartoon character Charlie Brown, 'I've developed a new philosophy ... I only dread one day at a time'.

Often job hunt plans are over-ambitious. You promise yourself that you will keep busy, that you will chase down every prospective contact, that you will leave no stone unturned. This plan may rely too much on early success, hoping that your perfect job is just around the corner, taking little account of fluctuating energy and confidence levels. While activity levels and numbers of approaches clearly matter, simple over-activity can wear you out with weak results. Other plans mistakenly

JOB SEARCH PREFERENCES

Activity	How often? Every week 3 Occasionally 2 Rarely 1 Never 0	How comfortable? Very comfortable 3 Comfortable 2 Uncomfortable 1 Avoid at all costs 0
Talk to friends and neighbours about my job search		
Email a summary of what I am looking for to contacts		
Go and talk to people about the jobs they do and the sectors they work in		
Ask friends and colleagues how they got their last 3 jobs		
Telephone to find out about a job before submitting a CV		
Ask for advice from former work colleagues		
Ask for information and advice from course lecturers		
Discover at least one job lead every 4 days		
Write speculative letters to organisations who aren't advertising		
Organise practice interviews with someone who has hiring experience		

Receive feedback on my ability to summarise my skills and experience briefly	
Video my practice interview performance	
Have a list of the top five organisations I would like to work for	
Have a list of 10 organisations I want to research in more detail	
Update my Linked-In or Facebook page to make it job hunt friendly	
Personalise my CV for each job application	
Analyse the top five items on an employer's vacancy wish list and match them in a covering letter	
Get out in smart work clothes at least once a week to meet useful contacts	
Keep a contact sheet of networking and other approaches close by at all times	
Keep a log of my job hunting activity and the time I spend on it	

believe there is some hidden scientific formula about the magic steps that will win you a job. In general, people report that they spend far more time job hunting during a week than they actually do (see Chapter 3).

So, how do we plan well when most people don't make developed plans, don't anticipate setbacks, and over-promise and under-deliver in their job hunt? The first stage is to have some kind of structure. Not everyone needs or likes structures, but most of us need structure slightly more than we admit. Having a structured plan means that you can see where you're making progress and where you're not. It means you demonstrate the right behaviours at the right stages and take risks in the right points. Planning helps you use your time well and wisely. You ensure that you take on tasks in the right order and at the right pace (see Chapter 3 for a more on timing). Planning means that you can see where you have made progress, and see what else you have to do. A plan means you can see the difference between random responses and proper market feedback. It means you can work smarter, rather than harder, at making connections and finding a job.

COMMITTING TO A WRITTEN PLAN

All planning is about anticipating bear traps rather than walking into them. It is also about staging activity in scheduled projects. Writing things down helps. Many people have experience of writing business plans, but don't write one for their job search. Career coach and blogger Leon Hendra writes:

> I write a business plan with clients, the business being the job hunt and often the next job. This includes business case, objectives, phases of the process, marketing plans / objectives, resources required, and timeframe; it energises the process for them and makes it seem like a more professional endeavour. I encourage my clients to take the plan to interviews – it often

ended up becoming the framework of a business plan for their next leadership position.

How are you going to devise a plan? Here's the good news. This book will do it for you. An overview of **Your Job Hunting Plan** is set out in diagram form on page xiv near the beginning of this book, and in more detail below. Each stage of the plan corresponds to a chapter in this book.

Your job hunting plan

Chapter	Job hunt phase	Description
1–3	Plan an effective job hunt	• Dust yourself down and do a quick check-up on the impact of joblessness on your confidence. • Sketch out a plan about how you are going to reach contacts, supporters and decision makers. • Get ready to start delivering positive messages. • Prepare for some big changes. • Talk your story through with people you trust. • Put appropriate record-keeping tools in place.
4	Catalogue your strengths	• Perform a thorough review of your skills and knowledge. • List other attributes that are likely to be attractive to employers. • Get skills feedback from friends and trusted colleagues. • Start collecting evidence for your CV.

Chapter	Job hunt phase	Description
5	Discover and decode opportunities	• Map what's out there. Start to draw up a list of target employers or sectors. • Investigate target sectors using desk research. • Seek face-to-face meetings with people doing jobs that interest you. • Interrogate employer needs and the typical profile of the people your target employers are trying to find. • Spot the language used to describe top candidates.
6	Write your draft CV	• Catalogue your experiences, shaping them into an effective document. • Design a tool which gets you into the interview room. • Use your CV as a back-up when having conversations.
7	Level 1 conversations	• Talk to friends and colleagues about your career ideas. Identify people who are tolerant of a degree of uncertainty and happy to help you with your exploration. • Gather feedback on your market strengths. • Gain a reality check on your ambitions.

Chapter	Job hunt phase	Description
8	Refine your CV message and start telling people what you can do for them	• Seek opportunities to talk through your message with experienced colleagues. • As you become clear about your target market, sharpen up (1) the Profile and (2) the Key Achievements section of your CV. • Learn to get your most important messages across on page 1 of your CV. • Practise answering the interview questions you don't want to hear.
9	Level 2 conversations	• Move into more focused explorations with Level 2 contacts who will provide a huge increase in information, connections and job leads. • Reach out to people who can get you in front of decision makers.
10	Develop a Plan B if networking is tricky	• If you're in a sector where networking isn't a suitable tool, make the most of other job hunt channels. • Continue talking to people about your career goals. • Make the most of formal job application processes.

Chapter	Job hunt phase	Description
11	Spot and target published vacancies	• Make your applications for advertised jobs as effective as possible. • Ensure your documents work without you being in the room to introduce them.
12	Organise your social media profile	• Set up a LinkedIn profile to manage your electronic 'shop window'. • Begin to use social media actively to connect with interesting people and push out messages to the marketplace.
13	Work with recruitment consultancies	• Pitch yourself to agencies, understanding what they can do for you. • Make sure your CV and opening conversations get the right message across. • Gain a secondary reality check.
14	Level 3 conversations	• Seek introductions directly to decision makers. • Make the best of job interview opportunities as they arise.
15	Pitch yourself to employers who aren't advertising	• Make direct approaches to organisations who might have a need but don't yet have a vacancy. • Get your strongest points across quickly without over-selling.

Chapter	Job hunt phase	Description
16	Job interviews	• If you've been shortlisted you're already close to a job offer, so don't talk yourself out of the job. • Focus on the issues that matter most to the employer.
17	Rejection, feedback and bouncing forward	• Review progress and revisit earlier stages. • Look in particular at stages that you have skipped over or given little attention to. Build on what is working.
18	Interrogate job offers	• Work through the key elements of the job offer. • Find out before you commit whether the job is going to work for you.

This version of the **Job Hunting Plan** gives you a road map of where you will be going and what you will be doing. You can of course dip into chapters as you need to, but be careful if you get too far ahead without doing some of the important planning work.

Can you accelerate progress? Yes, by working hard at some of the initial stages. Be careful though – read the section which deals with timing issues, including the dangers of going to the market when your confidence is low and your story isn't straight yet (Chapter 3).

What if you get an early job interview? Congratulations – you've got an early result. Don't blow it. Look carefully at decoding employer's needs (Chapter 5), your primary messages (Chapter 8) and interview techniques (Chapter 16). You might also consider getting hold of a copy of *The Interview Expert*.

CHAPTER TWO

Think before you plan

THIS CHAPTER LOOKS AT:

- Why job hunting isn't always as straightforward as it looks
- The dangers of reinventing the wheel
- Pushing yourself beyond passive behaviours
- Actions which will extend your job hunt
- Actions which will shorten your job hunt

JOB SEEKING IS OBVIOUS – I DON'T NEED A PLAN

Look at online careers discussions and you'll see a range of comments. Some people warmly welcome all tips and ideas, some respond that job hunting is simple common sense. Others are hostile, cynically stating that any positive-minded advice is too disconnected from the misery of the real economy to be valid. This reveals an important paradox in the world of career thinking, outlined in *The Interview Expert,* which described the irony that the world is full of people who say that interview preparation is all obvious, yet, even in a recession, employers complain that a large proportion of candidates are badly prepared for interview.

A similar paradox applies here. Job seeking looks easy. After all, how hard is it to send out CVs and application forms? Isn't it just a question of applying for jobs and keeping at it until somebody says 'yes'? Writing your CV, too, seems a straightforward task of cataloguing and filtering information. It's not rocket science, right? Yet, when I conducted CV research amongst employers asking them what they found most irritating, the most common answer was that job applications are not tailored in any way to the role, even to the simple extent of providing evidence which matches the employer's most visible requirements.

Taking time out now to review where a plan might take you can make a big difference. It can make the difference between an acceptable job and the kind of job that puts a spring in your step on a Monday morning. Practically, it can shorten your job hunt time.

There *are* barriers that get in the way of an effective job hunt. Some are external and forced upon us by the marketplace. The most important barriers, however, are the limitations we place on our own thinking. These limitations keep us stuck in one unreflective mode of behaviour, repeating mistakes in the hope that simple repetition will win the day.

These limitations are powerful enough to allow us to avoid reality. For example, even though candidates know that conversations with other people shorten job hunting times, they still hide behind their computer screens. They use LinkedIn as a reason to avoid human contact, not a means to encourage it. They pretend that social interaction in the job hunting process is instinctive extravert behaviour, not a learned technique that can be adopted by nearly everyone. By insisting that job hunting is logical, simple and hardly worth thinking about, they don't think about it at all.

We apply limits in other, subtle, ways. Candidates who find it difficult to secure interviews or job offers tweak and poke at their evidence like someone tinkering with a complex piece of machinery without any idea of the functions of various cables and switches. They often believe they need to transform everything. They restructure their CV several times and send out random messages, and when they continue to get poor results they start to believe that the market is too tough, too impenetrable, too arbitrary for any approach to work. The irony is that candidates in this position often only need to change a few small things to tip the odds in their favour.

Job seeking might look easy, and there's a lot of bland advice out there that makes it seem so. However, when you stand back and look at the activity, it's about communication, persuasion and influence. It's about convincing people you don't know very well to do something risky. It's less like filing a patent request, more like successfully launching a new product. Less like applying for a postal vote and much more like winning votes in an election when you're the outsider candidate.

If you are still unsure, just check out the difference it might make to think and act slightly differently. Talk to people who have found jobs. Give special attention to those who were unemployed for a number of months. Ask them how they achieved their final result. Then ask two questions: (1) 'what activities worked best?' and (2) 'what would you do differently next time around?' You'll often hear the answer 'I realise now I didn't use my time well at the beginning of my job hunt' or 'I wish I had realised earlier on how important it is to see people face to face'. You'll hear people regret the fact that they rushed to the market with a vague and slightly wounded message. Or they will say 'I see now I had my head in the wrong place.' They were swayed by arbitrary results achieved through indifferent applications for jobs they didn't really want. They will talk about time wasted online, saying 'I wish I hadn't used a scattergun approach and had focused on just two or three types of jobs'.

We would rather avoid thinking about how we do things while job hunting, and just get on with it, pretending that it's as simple as making an online purchase or applying for a loan. Any task which is about influencing and convincing others will always take more than five minutes to learn. Effective job hunting means thinking about how you will use your time most effectively, and knowing when it's too early (or too late) for some strategies. More than anything else, it's all about drawing on the collective knowledge of people who have travelled the path before you. If you insist on reinventing the wheel, it could be some time before you fall across the idea of a circle.

A job hunting plan is a framework, not a straightjacket. It needs to be flexible to your needs and adaptable enough to cope with the ups and downs the marketplace delivers. If there are parts of the framework presented by this book that you reject, rewrite or adapt to suit your needs, so much the better, but don't write off the experience of others.

Just as everyone has their own style when making new connections in life, job hunters have a variety of ways of doing things. Some never stray from their computer screen, waiting for something to come along. Those at the other end of the scale are natural extroverts so really good at 'getting out there' establishing relationships and broadcasting their availability. As this book will show, most job hunters are somewhere in the middle. People tend to use the same strategies, even the same CV and interview language, as everyone else. Most people adopt largely passive behaviours. They have occasional bursts of activity followed by quieter times when they lick their wounds, go offline and remember an urgent need to redesign the garden or put their CD collection in alphabetical order – distraction is a great way of avoiding a good job hunt.

YOU'RE GOING TO TELL ME THE SECRET IS NETWORKING, AREN'T YOU?

At this stage in reading the book you're looking for payoff. Is there a secret here? If there is, it's one that unfolds with commitment and experiment, not through punch lines.

And no, networking is not *the* secret. There are other vital elements. Knowing what you're looking for is vital, and so is getting your best message across quickly and efficiently. Yet if there is one activity that matters most in job seeking, it's connecting with people.

As this book will show you, this isn't about brash self-promotion or working the room with your business card. It's much simpler. You will renew relationships with people you already know. You'll find people who will inform, advise and keep your levels of optimism healthy. But your priority is new relationships with those people out there you haven't met yet who can open all kinds of doors. A good job hunting plan is going to extend the range of people you know.

Relationships matter for all kinds of core work activities such as selling, managing, influencing – so why shouldn't they matter most for job seeking? There is a difficulty, of course, as outlined by the comedian who said that 'the problem with beginning dating is that you have to do those two awkward things – you know, talking and listening'.

THINK BEFORE YOU PLAN

Many of us are attracted by careers where other people make decisions for us. Professions such as law, medicine and accountancy offer well-defined pathways. Careers within large organisations appear to offer stability and a well-defined path. Because of this we're very good at being passive in our careers – it's attractive, because you put yourself in someone else's hands, waiting for your boss, HR or a headhunter to recognise your value and tap you on the shoulder. This is a bit like waiting for the object of your desire to make the first move on a date, so you don't have to take the risk of being rejected.

This passive behaviour will have a strong influence on your job search. Registering on job boards or with agencies appeals because you hand the problem over to someone else. Job seeking using your computer is tempting, if only because you can get going quickly without having to wait for people to return your call, or risking that slippery business of building relationships. Staring at your computer screen also has another appeal – *it looks like work.*

However, the reality is that passive behaviour rarely delivers results. Waiting around for your brilliant career to start is not a very effective way to succeed. So, take one very important first step before committing to your Job Hunting Plan. You need to decide from the outset not to be locked into passive behaviour. Instead, decide to take an active role in your future, opening doors as well as allowing them to be opened for you. Above all else, keep asking questions – you're more likely to have a breakthrough chatting with the person next to you at the supermarket checkout than by spending all day registering on job boards.

Of course you will need to use the standard electronic tools, and use them thoughtfully and frequently enough to maintain your visibility, but keep in mind that *job connections start by being human connections.*

Even applying for advertised jobs is relatively passive. This idea surprises people who busy themselves sending off dozens of applications each week. However, relying exclusively on this channel is like limiting yourself to buying only products that appear in shop windows and never going in to see the wide range of goods available inside the shop.

Being passive isn't just about sitting at home doing nothing and waiting for the phone to ring. It's also about *putting most of your job hunting time into things that don't work very well.* This kind of activity is easy, and feels safe. Yet you may be applying for jobs where you will be showing employers how good you are at doing things which are not easy, and how prepared you are to take calculated risks. If you're active, imaginative and persistent when looking for a job, an employer can see that that's how you will operate when you're in a job.

Some activities feel easier than others – filling in application forms is easier than talking to people you don't know. There are some activities which feel more like work itself – for example, spending most of the day at a computer screen. Some activities are more fun, some more intimidating. However, it's also clear that some choices are likely to provide a better return on your time.

International career coach Angella Clarke-Jervoise writes:

> Before you plan a job search strategy, learn what really makes you tick at work. Review your major successes and think about what you do well and what you enjoy. Explore lessons that have come out of work situations where you weren't fulfilled or adequately rewarded. Being aware of this helps avoid falling into the trap again – it took me three bad jobs to work this out and I'm a recruiter!

WHAT YOU CAN DO TO SHORTEN YOUR JOB HUNTING TIME

So, as we've seen, all too often in job hunting we're drawn to routine activities which require little brainpower and offer minimal risk. Low risk activity is passive – registering on job boards, submitting your CV electronically with a covering email, filling in online application forms. You can make it look like hard work, but the odds on this kind of activity shortening your job hunt are poor. The higher the risk of the activity, the greater its long-term results.

A plan should really be a plan, not a vague sense of how you're going to proceed. Let's begin by focusing on the actions which extend or shorten your job hunt:

ACTIVITIES LIKELY TO KEEP YOUR JOB HUNT EXTENDED

1 **Registering exclusively on internet job boards.** This will work for some niche technical jobs, but for most it's a great distraction. It looks and even feels like work, allowing you to tick plenty of activity lists. But the reality

is that at best you get a 5% return on your investment of time.

2 **Only making online job applications.** The problem with many online applications is that you're often unsure how many others are applying, how long the job has been advertised, or how the information you supply will be interpreted.

3 **Submitting all applications by email without a telephone conversation.** An email is quickly overlooked or forgotten, and attachments may never be opened. A quick telephone call can alert you to the key elements on an employer's shopping list, and plant one or two messages about your suitability in the mind of a decision maker.

4 **Sending out CVs at random.** Employers can quickly see the difference between wild shots, which feel unfocused and expressed in the wrong language, and targeted approaches which know the right buttons to press. Random messages fired at random targets will give you random results. It's easy to mistake these results for hard evidence of the impression you are making in the jobs market.

5 **Registering with agencies before you have got your message straight.** Agencies can be very helpful but have limited time and energy for candidates who don't know what they are looking for, or what they bring to the party.

6 **Sending out CVs without adapting them to the job.** Unfocused, general-impact CVs shout out the message 'any job will do!', but a targeted CV matches what an employer is looking for, sometimes point by point.

7 **Closing down relationships after effective meetings.** Had a good meeting? Tempted to send your CV as a follow-up? Reading and acting on a CV is a big ask. If someone *really* wants your CV, send it, but if what you want to do is

remind someone of what you're good at and what's at the centre of your job hunting target you can do that in 3–4 bullet points. Maintain focus on keeping the relationship going.

8 **Having a phone conversation where you could have a face-to-face meeting.** Just as a phone call is remembered longer than an email, a warm face-to-face meeting is remembered even longer, particularly if you send a follow-up message including hard evidence of how the conversation helped move you forward.

9 **Spotting deal breakers.** Gaps in your CV or other problems in your documentation can get you excluded early from any selection process. Learn how to present your evidence in the best light so you leave fewer reasons for your CV to hit the 'no' pile.

10 **Using up your best contacts too early.** People commonly cash in their best contacts far too soon (see Chapter 3). If you use up opportunities to talk to great contacts when your message is unfocused, you waste some great connections.

11 **Going off to find yourself.** There may be times in life when you do need to travel, volunteer for good causes, return to study or retreat into a quiet space to rediscover who you really are. Do these things because they are the right thing for you, not as a way of delaying the unpleasant process of looking for a job.

ACTIVITIES LIKELY TO SHORTEN YOUR JOB HUNT

1 Start with low-risk conversations with people who are (a) supportive and (b) won't mind if you come back in a couple of months with a different story.

2 Get started. Don't delay Level 1 conversations until you have a perfect script – they're meant to be experimental.

3 Don't make the mistake of trying to conduct your job hunting without support, even if this is just the encouragement and support of colleagues or friends.

4 Seek out objective feedback on your CV and interview performance early on, and outside the process. Don't use job applications as rehearsals.

5 Don't keep job hunting a secret. Tell people what you're looking for – you will be surprised who can help you.

6 Learn to talk about your skills and achievements – find your own style for getting your strengths across in a way that sounds natural rather than like selling.

7 Talk to people doing the kind of work you'd like to do – be inspired, pick up insider language, learn from their mistakes.

8 Start exploratory conversations, right now, the easy way – with people you already know.

9 Talk to contacts face-to-face in their workplace – your visit will be remembered and your name may come up in conversation weeks afterwards. In addition, you will learn far more about organisations by seeing them up close.

10 Commit, early on, to the reality that before too long you will be having conversations with people you *don't* know – these will take time, patience, confidence and technique, but will give you the best results.

KEEP GOOD RECORDS

Dudley Harrop has worked both as a recruitment consultant and careers specialist, and knows the value of keeping good records:

These lists are not passive records; they are active mechanisms for working your way towards that job. They tell you what you have done so far – some satisfaction in that. They tell you what still needs to be done – and what new opportunities there are as you add new contacts to your search. And they also give you a view of what's going on in the market – how many of your emails are acknowledged, how many CVs generate a response, how long after an interview do you get an answer, are you doing better with big companies or smaller ones? The key point is that these lists provide you with some sense of *control* over what can seem a complicated and daunting process.

Here are some suggested layouts for an effective record keeping system – an **Organisational Research Record Sheet** and **Job Hunting Record Sheets**. A4 versions of various checklists and tables from this book can be downloaded free of charge from www.johnleescareers.com/downloads.asp. See also the **Job Hunting Timesheet** in Chapter 3.

Organisational research record sheet

Organisational Research				
Organisation name	Website	Notes	Questions	Next step/ contact

Job hunting record sheets

Level 1 Conversations & Research Contacts

Name	Organisation	Telephone	Notes	Referral to

Level 2 Conversations

Name	Organisation	Telephone	Notes	Referral to

Level 3 Conversations

Name	Organisation	Telephone	Notes	Outcome/ feedback

CHAPTER THREE

Time things right

THIS CHAPTER LOOKS AT:

- Beginning with the right activities
- Why people rush at the market, and what happens when you do
- Understanding the impact of early meetings and conversations
- How much time should you put into your job hunt

WHEN DO I BEGIN?

You might think this is a rather odd question. You might assume that if you need a job you should begin looking for it as soon as possible. Let's look at a two very different scenarios.

Plan A – where job loss is on the horizon

Your job is coming to an end in a few months' time – plenty of time, you might think, to line up a new job, but you've got a lot of work to do before you leave and you want to ensure a good hand-over to another staff member. What people typically do in this scenario is to put some energy into complaining about being laid off, and a lot of energy into maintaining their work, almost as if they half believe that the job won't really be taken away. Any job hunt that is undertaken is often half-hearted, involving the occasional foray into job boards and applying for advertised positions. Since little effort or attention goes into job hunting, the results are low-key. These candidates get worried about the fact that their departure day is approaching, and how tough the market feels. Soon the first day comes when they are all day at home, and the phone isn't ringing ... Soon they're talking about 'lowering my sights'. Plan B starts to beckon.

Plan B – where you need a job fast

Here you've lost your job with very little notice and you need a replacement income stream quickly. Or perhaps you knew some time back that your job was coming to an end, and you've left it very late in the day to start job seeking.

What do people typically do? They rush into activity. They fire off a hastily-adapted CV, register with one or two agencies and job boards, and start chasing job advertisements. Great – activity. The problem is, it's unfocused, near-random activity. What happens when you rush at a job hunt?

● You're not ready for questions about CV content. You haven't rehearsed skill stories or achievement evidence.

● You're not ready for questions about why you are currently looking for work.

● You're unprepared for questions about the emotional impact of redundancy and bring all kinds of emotional baggage into the interview room.

● You have a weak answer to the question 'why are you on the market right now?'

● You're not ready for questions about your career story or where it's going next.

● Your CV is unfocused because it's a hastily-adapted version of one you used five years ago.

- Your CV places a huge emphasis on the job you have just left, rather than the job you'd like to get.

- You're throwing yourself at vacancies without the first idea of what employers are looking for.

- You're highly attuned to anything that smells vaguely like rejection. Even when it's a good friend who fails to return a call, you may feel they have let you down hugely.

Recruiters see these half-hearted applications every week – a hurriedly patched-up CV, and an interview performance that shouts out 'I don't know what I have to offer or what I'm looking for, but I need a job!'. You might get an interview, but it's far more likely that you will trip over difficult questions about your motivation to find a job.

THE REAL STORY BEHIND THE FIRST DAYS OF JOB HUNTING

Let's slow the process down. When you leave a job, even if it's for positive reasons, all kinds of emotions kick in. Your first Monday morning at home will probably feel very odd, especially if you've been in continuous work for some time. The phone isn't ringing, no one is asking for your help or advice and your self-esteem takes a nose dive. You may feel frustrated, bored or angry with your former employer. Even the most robust candidates feel some effects, and some experience a real knock to their confidence.

Recruiters regularly see candidates who no longer believe their own CV evidence; instead, they are convinced that they have little to offer the marketplace. Worse still, they live out this belief by making compromises very early, in terms of job status or work locations which were previously out of the question. You might think this happens only to people with limited work experience, but career coaches see this vulnerability in highly experienced candidates. Self-belief is easily dented, and in a tough market there is plenty of opportunity to hear the word 'no', and have negative thinking thoroughly reinforced.

Career coach Jane Downes writes:

> The biggest error is 'going public' without knowing what you want. The result is an inconsistent message being sent out to the marketplace: you can actually end up going down a route you don't want. Candidates also often under-appreciate their transferable skills. This leads them to think of themselves in terms of deficit rather than abundant potential. Put simply, they close off very real possibilities or opportunities. The trick here is to take a full inventory of your transferable skills and then be open-minded about how these can be useful going forward.

Careers specialist Steve Preston suggests: 'look for small wins so you always feel you are achieving something towards your goal'.

The risk, of course, is that from the first days of a job hunt you get into a downward spiral. You don't really know what you're doing and send out all the wrong messages so it's inevitable that you hear negative feedback, even if it's just 'we don't really understand what you're looking for'. Does this matter? You could say that it's inevitable that people make mistakes in the first few weeks of a job search. The problem is twofold:

1 Early rejection leads to increased negative thinking.

2 People remember your early job hunt performance.

Early rejection leads to increased negative thinking

Here's something odd. You will set yourself bear traps. You will do odd back-to-front things that actually seek out negative messages. Setting yourself up to fail, just a little bit, is a great way of feeding that part of your brain which dislikes the risk of exposure and rejection. You try something difficult to prove that everything is difficult, so you can retreat into your comfort zone.

One of the tricks we use to seek out negative data is the old 'I'm applying for this job for the practice' game (see Chapter 17). Another is to throw yourself at a particularly high wall in week one. For example, people approach busy recruitment consultancies with an indifferent CV and a message that essentially says 'I am not sure what I want, but please find it for me.' Unsurprisingly, the response is usually *we can't help you* or the slightly more helpful 'come back when you've got your head straight'. However, your risk-avoiding brain seizes upon this as hard facts about the job market.

When people spend a lot of time explaining to their friends how difficult the job market is and how they have had to trash all their early goals, often what they are really saying is 'I got things wrong at the outset'. If you put yourself in front of important people and then confuse them about what you're looking for, or if you try to run before you can walk, you will certainly learn from the experience, but you will very probably also reinforce any messages that are lurking in the back of your head which are telling you how difficult things are going to be.

Getting things right often takes just a little more care and attention, particularly about who you speak to early on in the process. It's worrying how many people mismanage phase 1 of their job hunting and then use that experience to rewrite a CV or seriously deconstruct their interview performance. As in any research activity, early data based on poor enquiry gives you very unreliable results. In a commercial research programme you adapt and improve, but for an individual conducting a job hunt this is often enough to convince you of one or both realities – there's nothing out there, and nothing works.

People remember your early job hunt performance

Family and friends often apply pressure suggesting that the only valid strategy is to *get out there* as fast as possible. So you decide to play your trump cards first, and approach the people who you believe are the biggest hitters – individuals who can short cut you from A to Z – recruitment consultancies, former colleagues and bosses, your best networking contacts, perhaps a number of employers, too. You put yourself in front of these decision makers very rapidly.

What happens? The chances are you don't get far, simply because you haven't thought things through yet. You haven't anticipated questions like 'why are you on the market right now?' or 'why did you leave your last job?'. You will easily be tripped up by questions like 'what *exactly* are you looking for?' You use up your best opportunities in the first month – at exactly the same time you're recovering from feeling low about unemployment. Just at that moment you're feeling your way tentatively towards some way of pitching yourself. Ouch.

Early appearances have powerful consequences. Picture this as two separate rooms in one large office block. In one room, you're scratching your head and wondering why a conversation didn't go well, and feeling rather bruised by an early sense of rejection. The market seems tougher than you thought, and talking about your current situation much trickier. Imagine the person you saw yesterday in another room, busy working. This decision maker could make a big difference to your future. What does she remember about you? If your name crops up in conversation with somebody else, what will she say? Perhaps you conveyed a sense that you are bitter, unhappy, confused or simply unclear. You might get sympathy, but you probably won't get offers or referrals. What gets remembered is that you have a problem and you are not ready to solve it yet. *The message you have left in that room is not a message you want to travel in your absence.*

Timing your return to the market means achieving a sensible balance between recovery and opportunity. Move too soon and you send out all the wrong messages, too late and you've lost energy for the task. If your experience is too raw, all people remember is your hard luck story.

Get disappointment and confusion out of your system before you put yourself in front of a decision maker. This is one of the most important tips in this book. If you're angry about the way your past employer treated you, talk your story over with friends until you've got it out of your system. Avoid talking to employers while anger or bitterness might leak out.

This sounds tough, but it's easier than some people think, because it largely requires the discipline of learning pre-prepared responses that dig you out of emotional territory quickly and shift the focus from past to present: 'When the organisation restructured for the third time that year my role went along with dozens of others, but it's given me a chance to think about the kind of role I really want to do. The reason I find this job attractive is …'

GETTING INTO GEAR RAPIDLY

However, don't use reflection as an excuse to wait for ever. 'Candidates often want a break before starting a job search,' writes Kate Howlett. 'If only they realised that it is normal for the search to take from four to six months – they are going to get enough time off for sure!' Some employers find it difficult to process candidates (from first application to start date) in under four months. Kate Howlett adds:

> Networking shortens and going abroad to 'find oneself' lengthens – the problems and questions are still there on return. I have also found that recessions shorten job search as it focuses clients' minds, they procrastinate less, are braver and get moving faster.

You may be lucky enough to find an exciting opportunity already on your radar. If an opportunity comes up quickly, don't make the mistake of believing that it's too good to be true. Even if you know you could do a lot more in terms of planning and reflection, if it's a job you want and you feel confident enough to take an interview, pursue it. Use the best CV you can prepare in a hurry, and do three things as an emergency fix:

1 Match your key skills and achievements as closely as possible to the job.

2 Offer three or four clear reasons in a covering letter why the employer should see you, carefully cross-referenced to the employer's shopping list.

3 Find someone to give you a practice interview which will tell you where you are in danger of failing to get a job offer.

HOW MUCH TIME SHOULD I DEDICATE TO A JOB HUNT?

Looking for a job should be your full time job is a mantra you'll hear all too often. For most people that's a slogan rather than a statement about reality. Let's deal with two facts about job hunters:

1 They spend less time per week job hunting than they think they do or report.

2 The longer they are unemployed, the less time per week they spend job hunting.

In *The Unwritten Rules of the Highly Effective Job Search*, Orville Pierson recounts a survey of unemployed job seekers in the USA where two thirds reported that they spent *five hours a week or less* in job search. Few people spend more than 10 hours a week, even though they have just left jobs where they have worked 40, 50 or 60 hours a week.

Why do people over-estimate the time they put into job hunting? Guilt will of course always make you feel you should be doing more, so it's reassuring to say 'I've spent all week just looking for a job …'. The reality of course is that some of the time was spent fiddling around with your CV, some spent on related activities like journey planning and filing. To get results start asking yourself two questions:

1   How many hours am I actually putting into job hunt?

2   How much of that time is getting me any kind of result?

Agree a contract with yourself about the time you will spend on productive job hunting, and how you will record that time. Get the balance right. Career coach Kate Howlett advises her clients to undertake 'three to four hours a day of well planned search then the rest of the day should be totally pleasurable.'

RECORDING YOUR JOB HUNTING ACTIVITY

How much time you need is of course highly variable, depending on how market ready you are when you begin. You will inevitably spend much more time at the beginning planning, reviewing and gathering information. When you are up and running you should probably aim to spend about 20 hours a week in *productive* activity relating to your primary goal of finding a job. That allows plenty time for travelling, family and all-important social and leisure activities – what's the point of increasing visibility in your professional world if you cut yourself off from social contacts? However, ensure it doesn't drain you so much that you look exhausted in meetings.

Record keeping helps you see activity and progress. The **Job Hunting Timesheet** below may help – particularly when you have started to understand the different stages described. Record your time approximately in terms of hours rather than minutes, but be honest with yourself. Share your activity levels with people who are supporting you through the process, and reward yourself for hitting target levels of activity. For example, you might treat yourself to a movie and a takeaway once you have contacted 15 people in a week.

Job hunting timesheet

Time breakdown	Week beginning:	
Activity	Number of people approached	Approximate time
Career review		
CV editing and checking		
Practice interviews		
Background research on organisations		
Admin and phone calls setting up meetings		
Level 1 conversations		
Contacting new people by telephone		
Level 2 conversations		
Level 3 conversations		
Direct applications to targeted organisations		
Internet applications for advertised positions		
Applications for other advertised positions		
Approaches to recruitment agencies		
Following up on job leads		
Follow-ups with decision makers		

Remember to use the **Job Hunting Record Sheets** (Chapter 2) to record the conversations you have and the connections you make.

CHAPTER FOUR

Catalogue your strengths

THIS CHAPTER LOOKS AT:

● The value of focusing on strengths

● Building on skills evidence

● More effective ways of trawling your experience

● Prompts to help you remember where you put your strengths into practice

---

WHAT ARE STRENGTHS?

Candidates bring to the labour market evidence which falls under a number of categories:

Skills	Study History	Qualifications	Training
Personality	Experience	Specialist knowledge	
Attitude	Motivation	Adaptability	

This material probably already populates your CV and application forms. However, it's easy to get bogged down in your own history, putting down things that are important to you, rather than vital to an employer. Strengths are pieces of evidence that perform a number of functions:

Strengths

- Are rooted in genuine experience, not a vague sense of your potential.

- May be combinations of skills, experience, know-how and working style.

- Reveal the way you are likely to operate in a new job.

- Are expressed in language that an employer finds it easy to tune in to.

- May make you distinctive, and will certainly make you memorable.

For example, one strength that is valued in the modern workplace might be described as *improvising effectively under pressure*. It's the ability to come up with creative, appropriate and timely solutions, either working against the clock or where there are other kinds of pressure, e.g. quality, sourcing problems, client dissatisfaction or competing deadlines. This strength is a composite of organisational and people skills, experience, creative intelligence, negotiation (and possibly several other skills and qualities). Where have you done something like this?

Any understanding of strengths must build on the important work of Marcus Buckingham (http://www.tmbc.com) who in *Now, Discover Your Strengths* makes it clear that a strength is not simply something you are good at, and a weakness is not the lack of ability to do something. For Buckingham a strength is 'an activity that makes you feel strong – it's an activity that strengthens you'. He points out that we are not accurate judges of our own strengths and weaknesses, but there are clear signs when you are using true strengths, including 'positive anticipation' of future activities and an ability to learn and improve skills quickly and enthusiastically.

This philosophy is strongly related to the idea of motivated skills – skills you perform well and which give you energy. You can even be motivated by imagining using them. These are the skills you look forward to using on a Sunday night when you are packing your bag for work. When we use these skills we may experience what psychologists call a sense of *flow* – an enlivening mix of concentration and fulfilment that makes time seem to move very quickly. (If you're interested in the idea of motivated skills and flow you might also find it useful to undertake the highly recommended online inventory *What Do You Enjoy?* published by John Whapham – see www.w3-therapist.co.uk/ques-intro.php.)

Many people assume that listing their strengths in a CV or discussing what they are good at during an interview is as easy as writing a shopping list. It isn't, because of the filters that get in the way. When you sit down with someone who has just started on the process of career change you often discover that they have a distorted picture of their own skill set.

Distortion could mean a certain kind of blindness (see my thoughts on filters below), often expressed as: 'I don't have too many skills' or 'My skills aren't very impressive'. Others do have a shortlist of their own skills, but these are often mixed up with personality attributes, for example 'I'm a good organiser, I'm a team player, I can think on my feet', and 'I'm a self-starter'. These are a good start, but the skills are still abstract labels rather than being rooted in experience. Others give a list of skills which is actually a breakdown of what they need to do in their current job.

SURELY STRENGTHS ARE EASY TO IDENTIFY?

Perhaps the hardest thing about looking for work in a tough market is feeling that everyone else is more employable than you. It's easy to feel that way when you find yourself up against hundreds of other applicants. Alternatively, you may feel very employable but you're just not sure how to communicate the things that employers need to hear to have confidence in short-listing you.

An effective job hunt is about looking inwards and outwards, in different phases – inwards so you really under-stand how you tick, and then outwards to connect your offering with the needs of the workplace. Looking at yourself initially provides some useful data, and a reality check.

'Strengths can be seen in many ways,' writes specialist recruiter Pauline Godley. 'Some people speak about selling or meeting targets as a strength, but equally being a contributing team member is a strength as well as being methodical in your work. Strengths also apply to how people cope under pressure and how they work on their own initiative, so examples in any of these areas will help less confident candidates sell themselves.'

Many people who have an aversion to self-promotion find it difficult to find the right language to describe the things they have done well in the past. Career coach Stuart McIntosh suggests you start by showing your draft CV to colleagues and peers and asking the question 'What do I do well?'. Obtaining a kind of mini-360 degree review will help you quickly grasp good examples of where you have excelled or significantly added to the job description. McIntosh adds:

> Then decide, preferably with the help of a friend, where these strengths are best applied – what job are you looking for and what are the job titles which apply to these roles? (Sometimes this means changing your current job title to what the market calls it rather than what your employer calls it, particularly true in the public sector.) You can find these job titles by looking at Reed, Total Jobs etc. (but look across the UK rather than just locally) and researching what jobs are of interest and what they are called.

TRAWLING YOUR EXPERIENCE

Few people start with skill lists when they write their own CVs. They start with experience, which is complex, sometimes messy, with fuzzy edges rather than clear boundaries between 'skill' and 'knowledge'. We start with stories. What have we achieved? What activities occupied us?

Start with stories that have some sense of an outcome. So, for example, it's always easier to talk about a task which had a clear beginning, middle and end than it is to talk about something you did over a very long period of time. Start to re-process your career into a series of mini-projects.

Record as many strength-related stories as you can. You can do this in a number of ways. One obvious method is to look in detail at each job you have ever done, working backwards in just the same way that a CV covers more recent jobs first. Another method is to give yourself broad categories (e.g. work, formal learning, personal development, volunteering, hobbies) and see what evidence comes up.

Open a notebook and write down all those skills that come up in the **Seven Steps** outlined below.

Seven steps to identifying your most important skills

STEP 1 – SKILL CATEGORIES

Recall times where you have you used skills connected with:

- INFORMATION (research, data, analysis)

- IMAGINATION (creating, designing, building)

- PLANNING and SYSTEMS (structures, processes, organisation)

- GROWTH and ENTERPRISE (making new things happen, being entrepreneurial)

- INFLUENCING PEOPLE (leading, driving change, managing stakeholders)

- DEVELOPING PEOPLE (coaching, training, mentoring)

STEP 2 – A GREAT DAY AT WORK

Think about a day at work when you were in 'flow' – in other words, you were entirely absorbed in what you were doing, time passed quickly and you went home feeling a 'buzz'. Slow that day down in your mind as if you were watching a video frame by frame. What were you doing? What skills were you using?

STEP 3 – THINK ABOUT PEAK EXPERIENCES

What were the most interesting roles or projects you undertook in the past? What was the best job you ever had? What skills were you using?

STEP 4 – THINGS THAT COME EASY

What skills have you found it easy to acquire? What comes naturally?

STEP 5 – THAT SUNDAY NIGHT FEELING

Imagine it's Sunday night and you are looking forward to particular activities and projects in the week ahead. What skills are you looking forward to using?

STEP 6 – SURPRISED BY ABILITY

Think about a time when you surprised yourself by doing something you didn't know you were capable of doing. What skills were you using?

STEP 7 – THE MAGIC OVERLAP

Write down any other skills you are good at *and* you enjoy using.

Look at all the skills you have recorded in Steps 1 to 7. If you could choose only one skill from this list, which skill energises you most? What skills would you like to improve?

BUILDING ON SKILLS INFORMATION

A presented list of skills is not usually enough to get a job offer. How and where you have used those skills is what matters. Expand on each skill you identify by using the **Skill Diamond**.

Skill Diamond

Using the Skill Diamond

- **Context**. Where did you use the skill? What problems were you solving?

- **Complexity**. Describe the complexity of the problem or situation.

- **Level**. At what level did you use the skill between novice and expert?

- **Style**. How did you use the skill in terms of attitude and behaviours?

Record your results from both the **Seven Steps** and the **Skill Diamond** exercises above in your **Experience Databank** (see Chapter 6).

TURNING SKILLS INTO STRENGTHS

When people describe their skills they often feel like loose-fitting labels. Candidates say 'I have excellent written communication skills'. This may be accurate, but sounds stilted, and implies: *like everyone else …*

Career coach Zena Everett says that candidates:

are too generic about their skills and are vague about their career objectives, saying 'I can do anything in marketing' rather than 'I really understand the 40 something woman and her retail buying patterns so am particularly interested in a role that enables me to use this expertise.' In this market you are being hired because you can solve particular problems rather than just because you are a generic good all-rounder. Think back to when you were involved in a hiring decision.

Did you say 'let's get a nice person into the team who has good office skills' or was it the more specific 'let's get someone in who is really good on the phone and will manage the team's diary for us'? Putting 'reliable and dependable' as a skill on your CV doesn't make you stand out from the crowd.

Skills come alive when you describe them as strengths. In practice, what this means is embedding them in a story which is not about the skill, but about you.

Think about communicating your strengths in two versions: Americano and Espresso.

- The **Espresso** version is short and punchy. It's sometimes useful when you are introducing yourself by what you do rather than by a job title. You might use a one-liner in conversation such as: 'I've been told that I write good reports in plain English, and I am really good at explaining complex ideas in straightforward language', which, translated into a bullet point, is a good CV item.

- In a detailed interview response, give the **Americano** version – strong but slightly longer, for example: 'Perhaps a good example of my written communication skills is where I was asked to produce a new promotional leaflet. Everything we had produced in the past had just talked about us and what we did. I decided that clients are far more interested in reading about their own problems, so instead of a leaflet we produced a book about best practice, full of tips and advice as well as a short summary of what we did. The booklet had to be reprinted twice, and we even had a waiting list at one stage.'

Prompts to remembering how you used your strengths in action

An effective CV contains assertions and evidence, and the best kind of evidence of your skills and know-how is contained in defined achievements. Learned as mini-narratives, they are also useful to answer interview questions.

1 Start with supportive friends and colleagues. Ask them to remind you of things you did well, where you have made a difference, and what you are like when you are performing at your best.

2 Go back through your work diaries and logs. Stop and remember projects in detail. What did you actually do? What were you capable of doing at the end that you couldn't do at the beginning of the project?

3 Look for times when you faced clear problems or obstacles. How did you go about solving the problem? Where did your strategy come from?

4 Look at projects or tasks where there was a clear outcome, where something changed.

5 Where have you learned something very quickly in order to get something done?

6 If you worked as part of a team, concentrate on moments where *you* did something.

7 Collect tangible evidence of achievement – numbers, percentages, margins and timescales always help, but your evidence might be a letter from a happy customer, an award or a good appraisal.

8 Give equal attention to times when you used 'soft' skills, e.g. communicating, engaging, persuading, negotiating, coaching. Talk about what happened as a result of those interventions.

9 Look at the job description for your last job. In what ways did you redefine or enlarge the job?

10 Look for examples of times when you delivered more than people were expecting or went the extra mile to achieve the right result.

11 Look for times when you brought in new ideas or adapted something creatively.

12 Identify moments when you snatched victory from the jaws of failure.

Remember to look at achievements in your non-working life. It's often here that you find skills that are under-valued or undeveloped.

Careers specialist Malcolm Watt advises you to:

Build the stories which demonstrate strengths, and dig out the achievements within those stories. Remember times when you used these strengths and how you felt: the more you think about them, the clearer they become and the more detail you can add to them. This all helps build self-confidence and helps outweigh the feeling that you are selling something you don't really believe you have done.

Getting under the skin of a strength

- What was the task or challenge?

- What planning did I need to do?

- What obstacles did I have to overcome?

- What skills did others see me use?

- If I worked in a team, what did I do personally? How did I work with others?

- What was my best moment?

- How did I surprise myself or others?

- What would I do differently next time?

MOVING ON

How do you know when you have done enough to move on from this stage in the job hunt? You will have evidence of your skills *and* the broader picture, your strengths. You will have the beginnings of stories which will communicate how you used these strengths and what you achieved, rather than just a list of skills that feels disconnected from you.

CHAPTER FIVE

Discover and decode opportunities

TARGET TRACKING

Now that you've thought about your strengths, the natural next step is identifying organisations you would like to share them with. Rushing straight at organisations with your CV sends out mixed messages and often leads to early setbacks (see Chapter 3). However, this is not an excuse for sitting back and doing nothing. There is some important underpinning work to be done before your job hunting begins in earnest. Some of this is desk research, some involves conversations, but one of the best ways of using your time in the early part of the process is finding out more about organisations. Some will be stepping stones or simply good market models; others will eventually be targets for your one-person marketing campaign.

What kind of organisations and people? That depends very much on your agenda. You might be looking for a similar job in the same sector, or something different. Clearly the more variables you adjust, the harder the change becomes, so trying to change role and organisation *and* sector all at the same time takes some doing, and is more likely to lead to rejection letters and lack of progress.

CAREER CHANGE VARIATIONS

Same sector, same role

This is the easiest transition, but isn't always straightforward. In a declining sector, for example, competition for jobs can increase dramatically. Even staying in familiar territory still requires research – which organisations might jump at the chance to use your skills and knowledge? These will often be direct competitors of the organisation you have just left. Sometimes a well-pitched letter to a decision maker will be all you will need to get an interview.

Same sector, new role

This is also a *relatively* straightforward move, as what you are effectively doing is using job change to achieve an upwards or sideways move in your sector. Make it clear why you want a change of role, particularly if you want a lateral move. If you want more responsibility, your CV should show what you have done and how ready you are to take on a more senior role.

Same role, new sector

In some occupations (e.g. management accountancy or HR) it's relatively easy to move from one sector to another, since procedures and systems are often similar. In other words experience is what really counts – you can speak the code. The disadvantage is that employers and external recruiters may want to place you in exactly the same kind of role that you just left, but you may want something slightly different.

Investigate a wide range of organisations in your new sector of choice – this provides you with useful background information and helps you decode 'insider' language. This is vital for communicating transferable skills. The average candidate simply names these skills in the vain belief that a list of skills has some transfer value. Stronger candidates know that they have to describe these skills in the language the employer is used to hearing, *and* explain why their past experience is relevant, valid and useful. Making connections like this shows employers that you are serious about making the sector change, not just vaguely thinking about it.

New sector, new role

This is the biggest leap. On the positive side, we live in a society where people make this kind of change all the time. It's a leap because you are asking an employer to trust that you are making a sound decision, and that you're a credible candidate. It's therefore vital to communicate strength of purpose, show you've done your homework thoroughly, give hard evidence of your potential, and show very clearly how your skills and achievement match the employer's needs.

TARGET SPOTTING

How do you identify useful organisations and learn more about the sectors they operate in? To answer that, you need to increase your awareness of what's out there. Most candidates have very poor maps of the world of work. For many people career exploration is like navigating using a SatNav that hasn't been updated for 10 years – there are large blanks which should display road links.

You can start to fill in those blanks in two ways – desk research and live enquiry. Live enquiry begins to emerge as soon as we look at Level 1 conversations, so we can focus here on desk research. Past generations had to rely on business directories, but you can find a great deal of information at your fingertips when you boot up your computer. How you do this depends of course on the geographical area you want to cover. Most people have some limitations in terms of their preferred city or region. If you don't, you have a broader canvas (although do be aware of the limiting message that may be sent by the postal address on the top of your CV).

If you are looking in one part of the country, you can start with local newspapers and jobsites that cover that geographical area. National jobsites can of course be interrogated using town and county names. Some websites such as Jobsite.co.uk or Gumtree.com are set up to list jobs on a geographical basis. Use large jobsites just to trawl for the names of organisations. (At this point you may be protesting that this book generally discourages over-reliance on jobsites. This is true in relation to job applications, but jobsites are often a very useful way of spotting organisations who have needs and budgets.)

Many university careers services have websites covering employment opportunities in their locality, and you can trace nearby organisations through local employer directories and Chambers of Commerce. Finally, business libraries have access to good commercial databases of employers including OneSource, Kompass or Mint which can give you lists of organisations by size, sector, location and a range of other factors.

Previous generations had to rely heavily on advertised positions to give clues about work availability. Don't lose track of that channel – job ads, in print or online, reveal active organisations. The jobs advertised may not be what you're after, but at least you know who is hiring. Your task is to find out what drives that hiring need. There will be a variety of reasons why an employer might be a potential target for you:

1 The organisation regularly takes on new staff because of growth or staff turnover.

2 It has business needs or problems that will need solving soon, probably by creating new jobs.

3 It is a small organisation that is just about to expand.

4 The organisation or sector will be a very positive add-on to your CV.

5 There is a very clear overlap between what the organisation does and what you offer.

6 You admire the organisation's products, services or market position, or it inspires you.

Any of the above factors might be a reason to proceed further with your investigation. This preliminary research is critical. You start to understand the kinds of problems employers are trying to solve.

Desk research, supplemented with some well-placed conversations, helps you decode organisations further and understand the kind of people they are looking for. You don't start your job hunt looking for jobs, but for partner organisations. Good investigation gets under the skin of what it's like to work for a business, so it will ideally include conversations with past or present workers, providing essential inside knowledge.

When you have spotted organisations, find out more about them. Look at their websites to find out what sector they are in and what kinds of jobs they offer. Jane Downes advises: 'Select your top 10 organisations of interest and do some detective work around what they seek. Reviewing past job specifications is a great place to start here.' Look up key staff and find out something about their background. Review case studies the organisation offers about career development, or any news you can find about appointments. Look at the people who have been hired – what overlap can you see between their backgrounds and your own?

LANGUAGE AND BENCHMARKS

Give particular attention to the language organisations use to describe what they do and how they describe job functions. Some organisations, for example, put a heavy emphasis on technical language, others on the language of goals, values, customer experience, or social responsibility. Most describe work outcomes in ways that are unfamiliar to other sectors.

Don't just read job advertisements or descriptions. Scrutinise company reports and brochures. Look at press releases to find out the things that organisations are most proud of. Look particularly at the language that is used to describe success and lack of success. This might, for example, be clear where an organisation talks about standards that it works to. If there are technical terms used, Google them, and if they are still not clear, make a note to ask about them in future conversations.

KEEP A NOTE OF CONNECTING EVIDENCE

As you begin your investigation, start a notebook or computer-based record system to keep a note of organisations you have spotted, web links, facts, details and names of interesting people. Record your results using the **Organisational Research Record Sheet** (see Chapter 2).

While you are researching, keep updating your notebook with connecting evidence – in other words, pieces of information which can move you forward. This might be a connection to another organisation or another sector. It might be the name of someone you will eventually want to approach. It might be background information about an organisation's track record that will help you form future conversations. You will also pick up terms that need checking, and cross-references to other career paths. Keep a note of everything that looks as if it might help with future investigation, particularly if you have spotted questions that can only be answered by conversations with real people.

FOLLOW YOUR ENTHUSIASM

Research can be hard work and can hit set-backs, particularly where you need help from people who are sometimes too busy to return your call. Expect flat days. If you want to keep your spirits up while researching, focus on organisations and sectors that feel exciting. If you have some kind of energy driving your enquiry, you are always more likely to go the extra mile and overcome fatigue or knock-backs. If you are researching things simply because they look sensible, you are giving yourself plenty of excuses to stop looking.

HOW DO I USE THIS INFORMATION?

You might be wondering what the point is of having lists of organisations that don't currently have any vacancies. The point is that this information has value on several levels. The first is that you start to have a sense of what is within reach – real organisations with real needs rather than just an abstract idea about things that are 'out there'. You get ideas about who you need to talk to. You will start to collect useful information about the kind of evidence you will need further down the line when you are applying for jobs.

Even more usefully, research helps you to start to make choices about where you want to be, and where you can pitch your message. Try to spend more time and energy ruling things in rather than ruling things out. It's all too easy just to give an idea for career change the once-over and come to a quick conclusion that it won't work. That's not research, that's just a reaction. It could be a good gut reaction, but you still need to check things out properly. You will find yourself easily discouraged from taking things further by people who don't actually give you advice on a new sector, but simply offer activity-blocking statements like 'it's terribly competitive' or 'if you haven't got a degree you won't be taken seriously'. This is often a partial picture.

Research before job search provides you with better maps and helps you make better choices. The twofold aim of all career-focused investigation is:

1 finding out for yourself, and

2 finding out enough to allow you to move forward.

Finding out for yourself isn't just for those people who can't afford a research assistant. Firstly, if you paid someone to do the research for you, you'd only get half the results. This is because you are looking carefully to find out what happens under the bonnet, to get a real sense of whether career pathways might be right for you. This is as much about feelings as it is about facts. Secondly, finding out for yourself helps make you visible in a crowded market, as we will discover in the chapters to come. Being remembered as an enthusiastic enquirer is a great door opener.

Finding out enough to allow you to move forward reminds you that research is linked not to storing and cataloguing information, but to positive activity. The more your enquiries lead to real conversations, the more they assist. It's about finding out for yourself, which helps ensure you are remembered. Don't start your job search looking for vacancies – dig out the right employer before the job comes up.

Research is as much about how an organisation feels as it is about the facts. Career coach Ruth Winden stresses the importance of understanding culture:

> What has to be in place for you to do your best work? How does your preferred way of doing things fit with the culture of your prospective employer? Often people find out too late that they are in the right job but in the wrong type of organisation, because of a mismatch of ethos and working styles. Go beyond the image the company portrays on its website: talk to current staff and previous employees (who are often more prepared to talk openly); follow discussions and company communications on LinkedIn, Facebook and

Twitter; search on Google and consult sites such as glassdoor. com.

HOW DO I KNOW WHEN I HAVE DONE ENOUGH RESEARCH?

Research is a tool to help you move forward, not an end in itself, so it's important not to get bogged down in this stage and vital that you don't keep researching for ever. If you dig deep and ask around, normally you get some fairly big clues early on about choices that might work for you. The next stage is to draw up an action plan which will supplement your desk research with real conversations. We'll get there soon when we look at Level 1 conversations, but before then you will need to do some serious work on your CV.

CHAPTER SIX

Write your draft CV

THIS CHAPTER LOOKS AT:

- Choosing an effective CV structure
- Creating an Experience Databank
- Filtering, editing and composing a CV that gets you into the interview room
- How to design a CV if you hope to change sector

WHEN DO I NEED TO GET MY CV READY?

The vast majority of job seekers write a CV very early in the process and then tinker with it until they get a job. It never quite gets the message across, and even after a job offer candidates are unsure which parts worked. 'Candidates rush into getting their CVs written too quickly,' writes Keith Busfield, Director of Anderson Yorke. 'It's their first big demand of an outplacement programme. What people really need is an objective and a strategy. Writing your CV too soon is missing the plot.'

Your CV will remain in draft while it undergoes some market testing, but you may need a working document ready at short notice. Level 1 conversations (Chapter 7) will help you fill out and shape your CV. Level 2 conversations (Chapter 9) will provide a market test so your CV is fit for purpose when you start applying for advertised jobs.

CV ESSENTIALS

Too many candidates rely too heavily on their CV to unlock every stage of the process. A good CV will persuade people to see you, but it won't get you the job. No matter how brilliant a document you prepare, even a top notch CV will have far less effect than an average programme of outward-facing conversations. There are many CV guides out there, often with conflicting opinions and guidance. Here is an overview which is designed to take away the biggest headaches of CV writing.

- **Start as you mean to go on.** Keep your CV businesslike – don't head the document 'Curriculum Vitae' which sounds old fashioned. Just put your name at the top in its simplest form – no middle names, no letters after your name.

- **Think of initial impact.** An initial decision is made about you in the first 50 words, a firm decision in the first half page. Give more attention to the first half page than any other part of the document.

- **Say the things that matter fast.** Early on, while you've got the reader's attention, communicate the headlines – your background, skills and tangible achievements.

- **It's not a biography, it's an advertisement.** Don't overwhelm the reader with evidence, particularly if it's a series of chopped up job descriptions. A CV is there to communicate a handful of ideas, not your life's work. Give the reader a short list of reasons to invite you in.

- **Work to the shopping list.** Match your CV to the top five or six wants on the employer hit list.

- **Use a flexible but effective formula.** Write a profile and a series of high impact achievement bullet points (see 'The Hybrid CV' below).

- **Think impact.** Make it look good, with plenty of white

space and bullet points of varying length to ensure it's easy to read.

- **Avoid the 'so what?' factor.** Don't list duties which are obvious and entirely predictable from your job title, and don't list skills which make you sound like somebody much more junior.

- **Lead with the right language.** Avoid long paragraphs which will never be read. Use bullet points which begin with action verbs (e.g. 'led', 'initiated', 'managed').

- **Emphasise qualifications only if it makes a difference to getting shortlisted.** Otherwise list them deeper in the document and give far more emphasis to skills and experience.

- **Don't fall into predictable traps** – e.g. sounding out of touch with the modern workplace if you are an older candidate, or sounding naively proud of modest experience if you are straight out of full-time education.

- **Don't fuss.** Avoid acronyms, jargon, complicated explanations or details. Keep sentences short, avoiding sub-clauses.

- **Don't apologise.** A CV is no place to start justifying past decisions or actions.

- **Don't eulogise.** Describe, explain, but don't over-sell. Dudley Harrop writes:

  > Keep your CV profile brief and factual. 'Highly motivated and successful engineer; works well on own or in a team' is not a fact. It's your opinion of yourself, unlikely to be unbiased. Whereas 'Qualified chartered accountant with 15 years' experience in packaging sector' – is a fact and is information the reader wants to know.

- **Avoid features which worry the reader.** Don't leave obvious gaps. If you dropped out of a course or job, provide a short and simple reason. Double check company and product names, dates, figures.

- **Don't go overboard** on information on jobs you did a long time ago. Dudley Harrop comments:

  > Don't include short jobs that add nothing to the overall impact of the CV. You might bundle a few of them together and label those years something like: 'Worked with a number of medium-sized companies to extend experience of retail.'

CV FORMATS DEMYSTIFIED

An Internet trawl will present you with a bewildering array of CV examples. How do you choose? First, find CVs that match the market and sector you're aiming to get into, and don't get distracted by CV examples which (a) only work in other cultures or countries or (b) are so novelty-driven, design-heavy or gimmicky that they just won't fly unless you're applying for a highly creative role (in which case ignore all rules and be original). For 90% of job seekers a conventional format will work. See your choices on page 61.

So, how to choose? If agencies always offer you the same kind of job you did in the past, you've already discovered one major limitation of the Chronological CV. If you've tried the Functional CV you may not have received any feedback at all, because they are often ignored. A Profile-led CV might work well, depending on how well the profile is written, but can also irritate some employers.

There is, in my experience, only one format which works well in situations where you require a *handover message* – what you would say if you were in the room, handing the document across. You might say something like: 'before you read this, let me tell you a couple of things …'. The problem is that you probably won't be in the room, so you have to design a document that works without your verbal handover. This is why, if you want to make a career change, you'll probably need to begin with a profile.

CV FORMATS

FUNCTIONAL	PROFILE-LED	CHRONOLOGICAL
Lists key themes, skills or competences and offers examples under each heading taken from various parts of your history.	Starts with an opening paragraph which explains and emphasises key characteristics. May be followed by a Functional or Chronological format.	Without any summary information, lists your work history, job by job, usually with the most recent job listed first.
Pros: Useful if your transferable skills are not evident and if previous sectors/ job titles don't help you move forward.	**Pros:** Focuses the mind of the reader before they read your detailed history; often required if you want to change sector.	**Pros:** Uncluttered, and can be all you need if you want the same job again or the next obvious job up the ladder. Often preferred by agencies.
Cons: Disliked by many HR staff and most recruiters because it's difficult to work out your actual history.	**Cons:** Hard to write, often comes across as over-selling or unconvincing self-praise.	**Cons:** You will be pigeon-holed by the most recent job on your CV.

FORMAT AND IMPACT

There are many urban myths about how quickly a CV gets read. Experienced recruiters object to the idea that a CV is read in 30 seconds, and the best ones look at every detail. However what is uncertainly true is this: *a selector will have made critical decisions about you about half way down page one.*

Here's a simple test for your CV. Imagine you had it with you at a social gathering. A stranger asks you to tear off and give him just the first third of the first sheet. Would that stranger have enough information to spend the rest of the evening telling people what you have to offer? That's the part of your CV that gets read in detail. Keep your CV to an absolute maximum of three pages (two is better), but focus all your attention on the first half of page 1. This piece of information trumps all other CV advice, and helps you decide on which CV format to use.

Which format should you use? Cheat. Take the best of all formats and combine them in a structure which shapes a decision maker's thinking in the first 30 seconds. The opening section therefore needs to provide a clear picture of where you fit into the world of work, what you do well, your key skills and experience, and your track record. There may be other refinements, but in general that's about it. The **Front-Loaded CV** ensures that your CV hands itself over when you are not in the room, and gets the reader to make the decision 'this is someone we ought to see' in the opening seconds.

(See also the example CV material downloadable free from www.johnleescareers.com)

FRONT-LOADED CV-PAGE 1

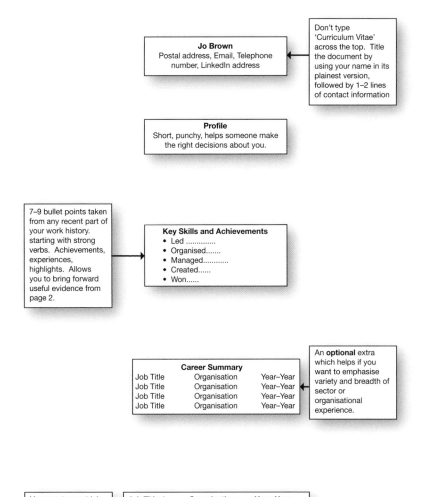

Don't type 'Curriculum Vitae' across the top. Title the document by using your name in its plainest version, followed by 1–2 lines of contact information

Jo Brown
Postal address, Email, Telephone number, LinkedIn address

Profile
Short, punchy, helps someone make the right decisions about you.

7–9 bullet points taken from any recent part of your work history. starting with strong verbs. Achievements, experiences, highlights. Allows you to bring forward useful evidence from page 2.

Key Skills and Achievements
- Led ....
- Organised.......
- Managed............
- Created......
- Won......

An **optional** extra which helps if you want to emphasise variety and breadth of sector or organisational experience.

Career Summary

Job Title	Organisation	Year–Year
Job Title	Organisation	Year–Year
Job Title	Organisation	Year–Year
Job Title	Organisation	Year–Year

Your most recent job appears towards the bottom of page 1, particularly if the role is not one you want to repeat.

Job Title 1   Organisation   Year–Year
1–2 lines summarising the organisation and the role.
Key achievements:
- Achievement 1
- Achievement 2
- Achievement 3
- Achievement 4
- Achievement 5

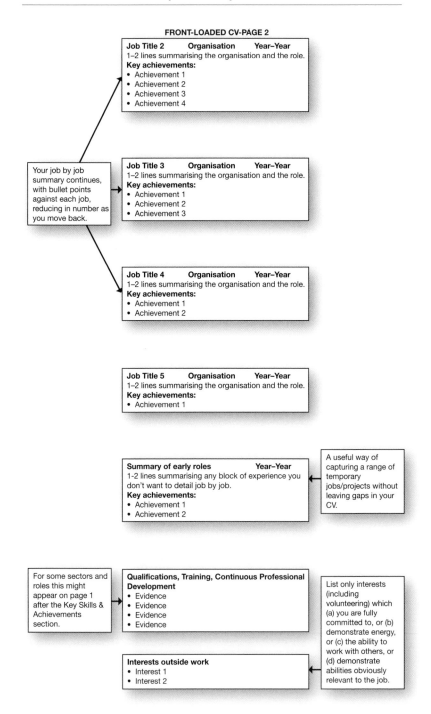

FRONT-LOADED CV–PAGE 2

Job Title 2   **Organisation**   **Year–Year**
1–2 lines summarising the organisation and the role.
Key achievements:
- Achievement 1
- Achievement 2
- Achievement 3
- Achievement 4

Your job by job summary continues, with bullet points against each job, reducing in number as you move back.

Job Title 3   **Organisation**   **Year–Year**
1–2 lines summarising the organisation and the role.
Key achievements:
- Achievement 1
- Achievement 2
- Achievement 3

Job Title 4   **Organisation**   **Year–Year**
1–2 lines summarising the organisation and the role.
Key achievements:
- Achievement 1
- Achievement 2

Job Title 5   **Organisation**   **Year–Year**
1–2 lines summarising the organisation and the role.
Key achievements:
- Achievement 1

Summary of early roles   **Year–Year**
1-2 lines summarising any block of experience you don't want to detail job by job.
Key achievements:
- Achievement 1
- Achievement 2

A useful way of capturing a range of temporary jobs/projects without leaving gaps in your CV.

For some sectors and roles this might appear on page 1 after the Key Skills & Achievements section.

Qualifications, Training, Continuous Professional Development
- Evidence
- Evidence
- Evidence
- Evidence

List only interests (including volunteering) which (a) you are fully committed to, or (b) demonstrate energy, or (c) the ability to work with others, or (d) demonstrate abilities obviously relevant to the job.

Interests outside work
- Interest 1
- Interest 2

FILTERING IN – BUILDING YOUR EXPERIENCE DATABANK

Before writing a CV, spend time collating evidence without applying any kind of filter. Grab a notebook and start writing out your **Experience Databank** – a list of the raw ingredients of your work history. Don't do this in the way you normally write your CV, job by job – write them down in the random order that you remember them. Keep writing down examples of positive experiences where you have used skills usefully and made something happen. Start by remembering those times when things went well at work – when you completed something difficult, when you received positive affirmation, when a plan came together, ….

Write down an entirely unedited list of highlights taken from any part of your experience, *including life outside work*. Don't choose what's good and what isn't, just keep writing, perhaps in the course of a long train journey. Think of it like reviewing videos of your past experience in seductive slow motion – keep looking for times when you did something worth pressing 'pause' for.

Leave the list overnight and add to it the next day. Ask friends and family to help jog your memory. Think about paid work, unpaid work, voluntary commitments, hobbies and interests. It might help to review previous job descriptions, diaries and work records, thinking of each job as a series of projects. Don't forget learning experiences. Use bullet points or short phrases which remind you of details which you will flesh out later.

Keep on adding examples. Your list will naturally be far too long and detailed for your CV, and that's just fine. This is your unedited, unfiltered database of the excellent, the impressive, the random and the ordinary. Don't start to edit it or extract from it until you feel it is complete, even if it runs to many pages. Keep racking your brain, making sure you include anything that could be useful – take special care not to exclude anything at this stage.

When you can't think of anything to add, record the list electronically. Don't edit, re-order or filter as you type. Your aim is to produce an unedited master list containing all your raw material. Save this file as **Experience Databank Master**. Keep this master list intact; you will need it in the future as your career develops.

FILTERING OUT

When, and only when, you can't think of anything else to add to your master document, you can start to organise information. Save your document as a new file: **Experience Databank Edit**. Now you can play with the contents. You might reshuffle the information so it is in date order. You might highlight different themes, or put information into different categories, for example all your achievement evidence which relates to people skills.

You might want to save a copy of this working file as **Databank for New CV**. Now is the time to relate your databank to the skills and attributes required by jobs you will be chasing. If it's just one job in your sights, that's straightforward – match carefully. If you are looking at a range of roles, think about the cluster of information which is likely to impress most – knowledge, strengths, experience and achievements. At this point you may need to get help from a career coach or someone who has experience of short-listing evidence you should exclude or include.

When reviewing material, ask 'so what?' – what looks routine and ordinary? What evidence makes you look like someone three rungs below you in the organisation? What listed skills are taken for granted in someone at your level and therefore carry no weight (e.g. a senior sales manager listing skills in Word and PowerPoint)? Some phrases make you sound like someone straight out of full-time education. The table below sets out the top CV clichés most likely to get you binned.

THE CV CLICHÉS YOU'RE TEMPTED TO USE	WHAT AN EMPLOYER IS THINKING
'Highly motivated'	*Why wouldn't you be? Why are you making this bland statement rather than showing me hard evidence?*
'People focused'	*Really? Or do you just like chatting with your friends at work?*
'Committed'	*Yes, so is every other candidate. Is there any evidence of this in your CV?*
'Commercial'	*What does this word mean to you? Have you thrown it in because it sounds good?*
'Dynamic'	*Really? Will we experience a powerful force in the interview room, or just someone who makes a lot of noise?*
'Results-oriented'	*Getting half way out of the cliché box, but could still be meaningless jargon. Where's the evidence?*
'Enthusiastic … Energetic'	*Sounds like someone with very little work experience …*
'Flexible'	*Could be useful, but is this code for 'I will do anything'?*
'Honest'	*Why would you raise the issue of honesty?*
'Hard working'	*… and why would you want me to start worrying that you won't work as hard as everyone else?*

THE CV CLICHÉS YOU'RE TEMPTED TO USE	WHAT AN EMPLOYER IS THINKING
'Conscientious'	*By whose standards? How could anyone challenge this?*
'Punctual … reliable'	*Now we're getting somewhere, but only if I see hard facts.*
'Self starter'	*What does this say about your past relationships with managers? How well do your respond to targets you haven't set yourself?*
'Team player'	*Meaningless CV noise. What kind of player in what kind of team?*
'Team player but I can also work on my own'	*Straight out of the CV cliché book. Covering all bases simply shows you're like everyone else.*
'Available for interview at short notice'.	*Too eager to please, possibly desperate.*
Interests: reading, travel, cooking	*Yawn … Why do you think I want to know this?*
References available on request	*Well, obviously …*

Next, highlight your strongest points – potential page 1 material. Ask yourself if there is any evidence you haven't yet recorded. Remember to copy fresh material back into your **Experience Databank Master.** The evidence you draw out will help your interview strategy as well as your CV, and being able to summarise your strengths will add sparkle to networking conversations. However, for now, just composing a master list will lift your confidence and start to get you focused.

CAREER CHANGE

Career coach Stuart McIntosh advises:

> Where there is a link between your previous career and
> the job you are targeting then the CV should be reverse
> chronological demonstrating your skills and experience in the
> context of the target market.

Where you are looking for a sector change you will be up
against candidates whose experience is more relevant, so think
carefully about the impact of your CV. McIntosh adds:

> Consider what a CV reader will think after a six-second scan
> or sift checking – is there a strong enough link between your
> job title/ex-employer name and the job being advertised?

If the link is weak, you may have difficulties, particularly if you
don't manage the opening part of your CV with great care. Use
the right structure and your CV can help you get shortlisted if
you don't have sector experience. How? Firstly, get a strong
feel for the job. Take any offered opportunity to telephone to
ask questions about the role (see Chapter 11). Ask around to
be sure what evidence to use, and what language to pitch in.
When you adapt your CV to the task of sector change, your
job is to actively help readers make connections between your
experience and the reality of the job.

Having begun with a thorough trawl of your experience you
should now have a draft CV to take you forward into your first
discussions. Later, you will sharpen up the primary messages in
your CV ready for higher level conversations (see Chapter 8).

Writing a CV to help you change career

1   Expand and explain past job titles to create the idea
    that you have done virtually the same job in another
    sector.

2   Mention on page 1 any background experience
    or learning that may help. Mention the names of
    organisations that will be recognised by a decision
    maker.

3   Provide a list of transferable skills on page 1, using
    terms that your new target sector will not only
    understand but find attractive.

4   Spell out ways that your study and training
    history have equipped you with relevant skills and
    underpinning knowledge for your target sector.

5   Lessen the impact of your actual career history by
    only including your most recent job on page 1 and
    putting the rest of your career history on page 2.

6   Finally, and most importantly, make sure that your
    CV profile sells the idea of career change. Don't start
    by identifying yourself through a profession or role
    label that you don't want to repeat. Do emphasise
    skills, qualities and know-how which help sell you
    into the role, and also spell out reasons why your
    background might be an asset.

CHAPTER SEVEN

Level 1 conversations

THIS CHAPTER LOOKS AT:

- Getting past your fears and suspicions
- How and where you begin
- How to spot your level 1 contacts
- The advantages of level 1 conversations

I JUST *HATE* NETWORKING

Most job hunters understand instinctively that there is great power in talking to people. They know, or have heard, that having conversations with movers and shakers is the most effective short cut. Statistically you are more likely to get a job through talking to someone you already know, or *someone you should get to know*. Talking to people of course isn't the problem, the issue is talking to people you don't know.

Most job hunters dislike the idea of networking. They fear the humiliation of asking for favours. They hate it when people don't call back or say they're too busy for a conversation. They dislike the idea of selling themselves. Some people even believe it's unfair or unprofessional. The word 'networking' raises all kinds of fears – are you going to have to 'work the room', give out business cards, deliver an elevator pitch?

Whatever it's called, it makes a difference. Even if you undertake just a few easy conversations, even if you only reach out to one or two people, even if you only reconnect with former colleagues and ask them how their jobs are going, you'll knock time off your job hunt. You can argue about statistics or outcomes, but you can't argue with the thousands of people who end up with a job offer because of a conversation. Leadership, Development and Team Coach Jo Bond writes:

> Unless you plan to live a hermit's life then an aversion to networking will negatively impact virtually any job you tackle. All networking means is talking with other people to gather information, advice, ideas, suggestions, recommendations, referrals to others, etc. It involves asking questions and actively listening to the responses you are given. It does NOT mean overtly asking for a job.

The first mistake is to believe that conversations will be primarily about *you*. The focus should be the person you're talking to. You'll learn a huge amount by asking questions such as 'how did you get into this line of work?' and 'what's changing in this sector?' Even the question 'what do you enjoy about your job?' can provide great ammunition for interviews. When the conversation inevitably turns to you, talk briefly and clearly about your experience, what you do well, and what you're looking for. No cheesy one-liners or slick pitch is required, just two or three quietly rehearsed sentences.

Therefore the reason for these conversations isn't self-promotion, but organised discovery. Keith Busfield asks:

> I wonder how many people understand true networking. It's about talking to people in any situation and finding ways of getting on with them. If you're unsure whether you will be able to network, you're not asking the right questions, which are 'is it really important? Do I really need to do it?' Be clear about the outcomes, then find a style of networking that works for you. Go to networking events, but if you're not

good at talking to people you don't know, volunteer to help run the event, handing out coffee or name badges. Finding ways of helping people gives you a great reason to talk to them. Don't call it networking as that's a big, frightening word – think of it as mutually beneficial conversations.

WHO DO I TALK TO?

Classic advice on beginning networking often invites you to draw a circle and write in it the names of everyone you have a professional relationship with, including your accountant, dentist, doctor and vet. This is in fact a random list of names of people who may be entirely unhelpful and unsuitable choices for level 1 conversations.

We need a new word to describe this activity – a mix of investigation, low-key broadcasting of your message, and plain old asking for help. Call it *catching up with friends*. Start here, because friends will give you plenty of support and will tolerate changes of direction. Next time you meet a friend for coffee, structure the conversation just a little more than normal. You could start by asking someone to review your work experience, reminding you what you're good at, and what you've achieved. You could talk about ideas for what you'd like to do next, and the kind of people you'd like to meet.

Career coach Ruth Winden writes:

There is a misconception that to be a good networker, you have to be outgoing, gregarious or even jovial. Far from it – if all professionals were extroverts, networking would turn into a pretty exhaustive affair. In fact, introverts have two distinct advantages when it comes to networking: they are good listeners and they think before they speak! Introverted networkers don't need to learn to network, they need to play to their strengths and engage with people one-on-one, have meaningful conversations, and build strong connections over time.

Level 1 conversations are about the gentlest form of networking, and anyone can do it. Most people will not only benefit from these conversations, but enjoy them. You'll be talking to people you already know and trust, in a way you've never done before. This approach helps avoid mistakes that will feel like set-backs. Like the cold rebuff you get when you start a phone call saying 'you don't know me, but ....' Like approaching high level contacts too early in the process – when you're still feeling bruised by redundancy and you don't know what you're looking for. Why give people the opportunity to say 'not now' or plain 'no' when you're aware how much these will set you back?

Starting with the level 1 conversations will give you the confidence to get really good at these structured conversations and within about a month or so you will feel ready to move onto that all-important next tier of new people in new organisations.

STARTING WITH THE RIGHT PEOPLE

How do you know if someone is a potential level 1 contact?

- They are easy to approach and easy to talk to.

- They are naturally positive and supportive.

- They have at least a few good ideas for you.

- They will be happy to remind you of your strengths.

- They are the kind of people you can go back to in the future with adapted or even contradictory ideas.

- Some of these people will have obvious contacts (and some won't).

Those are the must-have elements. In addition, it's great to talk to people who might actually know something about the job market or what employers are doing, and someone who is capable of introducing you to new people. So only talking to people who are retired, for example, may not move you forward as fast as talking to people who are currently in work, but don't rule anyone out.

Finally, they are close at hand. That doesn't necessarily mean they live around the corner. What it means is that when you look at the picture of what is 'out there' in terms of work and opportunity, they are in the foreground. Too many people try to scrutinise the far horizon for great contacts, approaching people cold, and miss out on the brilliant connections who are one easy phone call away.

They are the people who will usually ask how you are, and how your family's doing. They are the kind of people you can trust with an honest account of how you feel about being made redundant. These individuals can be trusted with some important questions and ideas and if you go back to them three months later with a change of plan, they will forgive that.

Why approach these people at all? They possibly know you too well to give you cold, objective feedback on your CV or interview techniques, but they can do so much more. They are natural encouragers, positive minded people who can remind you of what you have done well, and help keep your energy levels up in the weeks ahead. You may feel you know all about them and everything they offer, but they will be natural ambassadors and agents – they will naturally give you a call if they come across a job that suits you.

So, pick up that phone. Your conversation might begin 'this is going to sound a little strange …' or 'I'm going to get this wrong, but …'. The real test of whether you are approaching the right people is that it won't matter. Level 1 contacts have your interest at heart, so they're tolerant enough to cope with mistakes and reversals. When you pick up the phone to speak to them you know that you can just begin a conversation, and you don't need to prepare a script of what you will say.

Start with these small steps. Spend anything from two to six weeks talking to people who are encouragers, asking them questions you've never asked before about people they know. Try this with friends, relatives, neighbours, even family – you'll be surprised at the ideas and great connections they come up with. Don't go home without asking the question 'who else should I be talking to?'

REMIND ME – WHY AM I DOING THIS?

The advantages of working for a few weeks with just level 1 contacts are:

- You tell your 'why I am on the market' story a few times and get any emotional colouring out of your story.

- You gain confidence from hearing positive feedback.

- You get used to talking about yourself and start to learn to talk about what you have to offer.

- You can try out ideas for new career directions, even off the wall ideas, without being knocked back.

- You can try out ideas for a job hunt strategy, and share your job hunting plans.

- You will receive advice, tip-offs, useful information and background research.

- You can start to formulate answers to more demanding questions about your career intentions.

- You can start to collect warm introductions to level 2 people.

- You start to 'talk out' your leaving story and get it out of your system before getting in front of decision makers.

- You will come across useful information and contacts.

- You will get very little resistance and few knock-backs.

On the last point, exercise some caution. Some of your level 1 contacts may indeed be easy to approach, but they may also be the kind of people who will pour cold water on your best career ideas. There are plenty of people out there who are happy to remind you to be 'sensible' or want to tell you how difficult the job market is right now. Some of them may have had their own negative experiences. Talk to people who have useful information and contacts (not forgetting that people will always have more ideas here than you think). The time for a hard reality check will come later; for now seek out people with a positive outlook.

Be honest about what you're asking for – make it clear that you are setting up brief conversations with a range of people to find out what goes on under the bonnet in a particular sector. Ask people for things they are happy to deliver – not CV advice or a job interview, but a good conversation about the world the post holder knows well. And thank people properly. Career coach Julian Childs writes:

> People forget appreciation courtesies and to keep contacts informed of their subsequent progress, especially as a direct result of suggestions, advice and introductions received. Basic sincere human courtesies go a long way, whilst their absence slows things down.

HOW DO I BEGIN?

In a sense, if you have to ask that question it may be because the people you intend to approach are not true level 1 contacts. If you have to plan what you have to say at the beginning of a meeting, the people you have in mind may well be level 2 or 3 contacts. At this stage when you pick up the telephone to phone Jane, and if she is really a level 1 person, you don't have to plan anything beyond 'Hi Jane, it's me. Fancy a coffee tomorrow?' When you move up the networking slope you need to become progressively more focused on what you say – when asking for a meeting, and when the discussion starts.

With level 1 people, however, it doesn't matter how you set the meeting up or how you start ('Listen, this is going to sound like a jumble sale of ideas ...' or 'I'm going to tell you how I feel about being unemployed, and I'm going to swear quite a bit').

USE A SIMPLE STRUCTURE

Before you do meet your supportive and loyal friend Jane, think about putting a game plan in place. This is something you are going to be entirely transparent about, so tell your friend what you're doing. If your friend has issues to discuss, agree to split the time equally.

Having some kind of loose agenda helps. It makes sure that the conversation doesn't become just a chat, and it helps cover the things you most need at the moment. Don't over-formalise things, but your friend probably won't mind if you start by saying 'Can I pick your brain?' and pull out a notebook. It will help you to have a simple outline and script in your head, for example:

Outline script for a level 1 conversation

Overview	Jane, it would be great if you could help me with my job search today. I'd love to see what ideas you have for people I could talk to.
Leaving story	First of all though, can I just tell you why I'm on the market at the moment and see how that sounds to you?
Strengths	Fantastic, thank you. I'd also like to think about what my best skills are. Knowing my experience as you do, what would you say my strengths are?

Achievements	What would be good examples from my experience I could use as achievement stories (or 'let me try out this story on you and see how it sounds …').
People connections	Brilliant advice, thanks Jane. Now, as I mentioned, I want to start talking to people. So, for starters, who do you think I should be talking to?
Industry focus	I wonder – do you know anyone who works in interior design?
Final check	Who else should I be talking to …?
Next steps	These people sound great. I am not rushing at new contacts just yet. It's a big ask, I know, but when I'm ready in a week or two, would you kindly contact these people and ask if they will see me?

HOW LONG SHOULD YOU HAVE LEVEL 1 CONVERSATIONS?

Everyone needs them. Even the most confident career changers need level 1 conversations just to ensure that they feel OK and sound OK about the process, and to seek a word of advice from good friends before they put themselves in the hot seat of a job interview.

Most people, particularly those who believe they can throw themselves straight into the job market, need quite a few level 1 conversations. That's one of the reasons why there is a slight delay factor in picking up on recommended names and connections. If there wasn't, you could easily be talking to level 2 or 3 people within a week of starting. Use level 1 as a practice zone and a safety area.

How do you know if you've done enough? Here are some guidelines:

- You've got a short, upbeat and safe statement for any question asking about your leaving story.

- You're starting to talk confidently about your 'offer'.

- You have some good names and connections in your notebook, and all you need is the green light of an introduction.

- You have a clear structure in your head for a confident level 2 conversation.

TAKING THINGS TO LEVEL 2

Keep on asking people you know for information, ideas and connections, but once you find level 1 conversations easy, take the first step. Go back to one of your friends and say 'remember you offered to introduce me to Dave Smith ...? If you could do that now, that would be brilliant'. If you catch your friend at a busy moment they may just want to give you an email address or telephone number, but this is less likely to be effective. Follow up on introductions and as you start to talk to people you don't know, the breakthroughs begin.

Before that stage we will build on the results of your early conversations and polish your CV.

CHAPTER EIGHT

Refine your CV message and start telling people what you can do for them

---

THIS CHAPTER LOOKS AT:

- Building on feedback from level 1 conversations
- Communicating your best evidence
- Focusing on key skills and achievements
- Writing your CV profile
- Why you may never need a CV

LEARNING FROM LEVEL 1 CONVERSATIONS

In your easy-access meetings at level 1 you discover what it feels like talking to people about the world of work that they know. You begin to learn how to make open-ended enquiries that sound like just that – enquiries, not veiled requests for job interviews. You are learning how to seek help without asking for something difficult or embarrassing. Level 1 conversations get you used to talking about yourself and your 'offer'. Your offer is communicated in your CV, in cover letters, in application forms, during level 2 conversations and at interview. And you learn to shape it in such a way that it will be remembered, and passed on.

THE PROBLEMS OF SELLING YOURSELF

When a friend with similar work experience shows you her CV it tends to look good to you. Someone else's experience can easily feel more impressive, more *valuable* than your own.

While some people are happy making outrageous – if not exaggerated – claims about their abilities, most find this uncomfortable. Candidates often say that they intellectually know that they need to sell themselves, but anything that feels like selling feels wrong. This means that many candidates under-communicate their strengths and experience. Describing your strengths feels self-centred or plain wrong to many. Even confident interview candidates and public speakers will tell you that they have a little voice in their head saying 'Does any of this make sense?' at least half the time, accompanied by 'Do I look stupid?', 'Do I sound pushy?', 'Am I bragging?', 'Am I faking it?'

These self-checking mechanisms are often very helpful. When they work well they will tell you the right moments to keep silent, or to dial things back if you are being too forthright. However, excessive self-checking can prevent you spotting suitable evidence from your past, and disable you from talking about what you do best.

SELECTIVE USE OF INFORMATION

Think of all the hundreds of photographs you have on disc of family and friends. Most will never get printed, but if you decided to set out a framed collection of pictures which say something important about people you're close to, how many would you choose? Perhaps 10, 20, 30? You'd make a small, representative selection. You probably know already which pictures they would be. How many of them would you grab if your house was on fire?

Your life contains many moments, many pieces of evidence. Some are purely personal, some make good stories, some are very special to you. A small proportion of those moments will become evidence you use in a job hunt. Imagine all those pieces of evidence piled up like a pyramid made of small stones – a pyramid of information. The base of the pyramid contains the largest quantity of material. This is your unfiltered experience, years of it, one day after another. By using the **Experience Databank** (see Chapter 6) you use active memory to catalogue that experience into something which is accessible and starts to make sense. Then you began to filter, to draw out the biggest and brightest pieces of evidence. As the pyramid narrows, you become selective. You will extract enough for a CV, so it contains no more and no less than you need. Later at interview you will filter again, because you will probably only have a chance to talk about 30–50% of the items in your CV.

You will, however, win the interview with a very small amount of information taken from the very tip of the pyramid. This is transmitted in:

- your CV profile;

- CV key skills and achievements;

- summary messages you communicate by email;

- quick summaries you present verbally in conversation.

You might leave this messaging to chance. Five-star job seekers know that's a dangerous game. Composing, testing, refining and perfecting these messages is one of the key steps you can take to shorten your job hunt time.

WHERE THE READER'S EYE RESTS

Research published by www.theladders.com used an eye tracking technique to analyse how online CVs are read, suggesting that recruiters spend just six seconds on their initial 'fit/no fit' decision. The research claims that recruiters spent almost 80% of their review time on the following data points:

1   Name

2   Current job title and company

3   Previous job title and company

4   Previous position start and end dates

5   Current position start and end dates

6   Education

Beyond these six data points, recruiters did little more than scan for keywords to match positions. This research is perhaps not extensive enough to be conclusive, but is a good reminder that if the above key information is not readily visible your CV is probably not going to grab attention quickly.

GAPS AND PROBLEMS

Remember that a CV reader also notices what is not there, so be very careful of gaps and problems in your CV that will be obvious during a quick read. Some advice from experienced recruiter Pauline Godley:

> Always be truthful and fill in the gaps in your CV. The human mind is predisposed to thinking negative thoughts before positive ones, so to avert this fill in the gaps! Travelling and exploring the world is viewed positively these days especially if it was self funded. Learning how new cultures operate, finding your way around a strange country and getting back in one piece is not just admirable but many people wish they had the guts to do it themselves. We are now, as a species, more global in our outlook and this is a positive thing.

LISTING KEY ACHIEVEMENTS IN YOUR CV

Go back to your **Experience Databank** (Chapter 6) where you should have several dozen experiences listed, if not more. Now you are going to decide on the key points you are going to get across early in page 1. You may potentially have hundreds of pieces of evidence which might qualify as achievements, but now you are looking for headline items – pitching between seven and nine great examples in the hope that a decision maker will find two or three which are strong matches. The great thing about this section of your CV is that you can feed in evidence from any part of your history, including study or life outside paid work. You can also change the order of these examples quickly to match a role, or swap in new items without affecting the overall CV structure.

So, for example, after a profile your CV might include a list of skills and strong achievements, such as:

Key skills & achievements

- Deputised for the Department Manager at customer briefings.

- Organised and project managed a review of outsourcing costs, leading to savings of 20% in a six-month period.

- Worked to demanding quality control standards, exceeding targets for cost and efficiency.

- Consulted across disciplines to produce new online safety guidelines.

- Trained and supervised two graduate apprentices.

Or, for a more senior role:

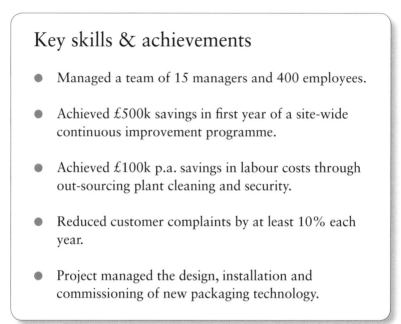

Key skills & achievements

- Managed a team of 15 managers and 400 employees.

- Achieved £500k savings in first year of a site-wide continuous improvement programme.

- Achieved £100k p.a. savings in labour costs through out-sourcing plant cleaning and security.

- Reduced customer complaints by at least 10% each year.

- Project managed the design, installation and commissioning of new packaging technology.

This section of your CV is read with great attention. The reader's eye is attracted to the left-hand side, so begin bullet points with strong verbs, adding concrete evidence of achievement. Remember other factors known to attract positive attention such as the names of major organisations or reference to products, brands, equipment or processes. Increase the chance of your bullet points being read by varying the length of each line and keeping sentences short.

WRITING YOUR CV PROFILE

Don't try to write your profile until you have composed the rest of the CV. This is the moment where you will decide on the information that sits right at the top point of your pyramid – a profile composed of three or four sentences captures your most important statements.

A profile can steer readers away from the wrong assumptions and lead them towards the evidence you want to highlight: experience of different roles, sectors and working environments, for example. Emphasise transferable skills by describing them in the kind of terms that an employer not only recognises but welcomes. Avoid using limiting job titles too early on – write about what you did, not what it was called. In the first 20 lines or so of your CV make sure you provide evidence which strongly matches the employers' wish list.

Employers dislike profiles if they are full of self-praise, but appreciate ones which say who you are, what you have done, and where you'd like your career to go next, which is one simple structure that works well. Here are examples of CV profiles that have worked pretty well:

1   An experienced IT programme and portfolio manager with a successful history of core system replacements and organisational mergers in the financial sector; underpinned by a proven track record of leading large IT delivery functions.

2   Values-driven public relations and internal communications director qualified to Master's level. An industry reputation for being strategic and creative with a real delivery focus. Proven track record in transformational change and stakeholder engagement and delivery of national and local media, public affairs, colleague engagement and community programmes.

3   A client focused research manager experienced in developing and managing research teams that deliver bespoke information across a wide variety of sectors. Ten years' experience of delivering quality information services which consistently perform on client satisfaction KPIs. With well developed management and influencing skills and a history of leading effective teams.

4   A design graduate with a wide range of customer

service experience acquired from a range of roles including hospitality, tourism, market research, sales and promotions, archiving, and previous volunteer experience working in a specialist wildlife centre.

Whilst none of the above profiles are the last word in phrasing, they have all worked to move four candidates forward, quickly, into interviews and job offers. Why? They have a number of features:

- They begin with a positive form of pigeon-holing often set at a tangent to each person's most recent job. Readers like to get a quick handle on the question 'what are you?'

- They reveal sector and skill coverage quickly.

- They don't waste time with too many adjectives.

- They focus on evidence which differentiates them from other applicants.

- Each profile points to hard evidence which will appear later in the CV.

- By the end of the two to three sentence profile you already have a strong sense of what someone does, their strengths and career highlights, and what they might bring to a new employer.

10 reasons CVs are rejected

In buoyant times employers may sift CVs into three piles – yes, no, and maybe. In tough times there's no *maybe*, and a very large *no* pile which your CV can hit for any number of reasons:

1 Your CV is not tailored to the role – either in terms of content (right skills and knowledge) or style (the

information is hard to find and not in language an employer finds it easy to buy into). Avoid impenetrable acronyms or jargon.

2 The first 30 words of your CV send out the wrong summary message – for example starting with a job title which limits your options.

3 Younger applicants tend to write far too much about their study history and qualifications and not enough about skills.

4 Avoid CV clichés ('individualist but also a team player'); focus on what you have done rather than what you think you are like.

5 Over-delivery is a major problem. The best CVs get your five to six most suitable pieces of evidence across quickly; the worst are full of irrelevant data.

6 Avoid sloppy or complicated language. Start sentences with energetic verbs (e.g. led, organised, initiated, adapted).

7 Weaker CVs tend to be a rehash of past job descriptions. Stronger ones reveal what you added to each role.

8 Employers are quickly put off if you over-sell your abilities or make too much of modest experience.

9 Back up any claims you make with hard evidence, quantifying your results wherever possible.

10 Don't list skills which could be performed by someone much more junior than you.

WHY A CV CAN BE A CONVERSATION STOPPER

Imagine yourself in the shoes of Michael, a decision maker working in a busy organisation. You had a really useful meeting with Michael this morning and you did well, communicating useful skills and knowledge. You get home and decide to follow up the conversation with a short, friendly email. You attach your CV. This is the last contact you have with Michael.

Many clients seek as many opportunities as they can to send out CVs to senior people in their network, often after good conversations. They are therefore often puzzled by the way their CV can sometimes bring the conversation to a sudden halt. A CV is a complex document requiring a relatively complex response. If someone specifically asks to see your CV, send them a good one, but don't assume that this will move things forward. 'Send me a CV' is often simply a courtesy, another variation on 'thank you for coming to see me'. Sending a CV when it wasn't asked for has an even more uncertain effect.

When a CV arrives you're asking somebody to do something which is demanding and problematic. You're giving somebody a task they are not comfortable with. Is your contact supposed to comment on your CV, give you tips to improve it? That means reading it in detail, which takes a good 10 minutes, plus the same amount of time again writing out comments. The second assumption quietly hiding within your request is that your contact will pass your CV on, with favourable comments, to another decision maker. This might happen after a Level 3 conversation (see Chapter 14). Otherwise it's unlikely on the strength of your CV alone. If someone is going to recommend you or pass you on to another contact, they will probably do so on the basis of a conversation alone.

All of the above scenarios mean that there are plenty of reasons why your CV will gets put into 'pending' which, in a busy world, means 'will never be read'. If any action is taken, the most likely thing is that your CV gets passed on to another decision maker who is just as busy and even less inclined to read it. Or it gets passed along to HR, which means that you now become a candidate in a detailed and possibly extended process.

SO, WHAT SHOULD I SEND TO FOLLOW UP AFTER A MEETING?

The first thing to send in response to any face-to-face meeting is a warm note of thanks. Somebody has given some time to talk to you. Send a proper handwritten thank-you card, ideally giving some indication of what happened as a result of a very good conversation. This action is considered an absolute must by *What Color Is Your Parachute* author Dick Bolles, who has advocated it in every workshop. It works. People remember a thank you card for months, if not years. If a conversation leads to something significant further down the line, including a job offer, write again. Keeping people informed of your progress and thanking them for helping you along is one of the things that turns functional networking into genuine and long-term relationships.

WHY YOU MIGHT NEVER USE A CV

It's interesting to see how many people manage to change jobs without ever producing or sending out a CV. These are usually people who prefer verbal communication rather than documents. They make relationships and build on them through conversations, either on the telephone or face to face, and always speak to someone rather than writing to them. As a result of being known, they find themselves invited to interviews and get offered jobs, without any documents being exchanged apart from a job offer letter.

While this experience is exceptional, you may well need your CV far less frequently than you think. The danger, in fact, is that you rely on it rather than having level 2 conversations.

CHAPTER NINE

Level 2 conversations

THIS CHAPTER LOOKS AT:

- Placing your chips wisely on the job roulette table
- When it's right to begin level 2 conversations
- How to get meetings without introductions
- Why level 2 conversations push your job hunting into a new gear

---

MOVING FORWARD INTO BREAKTHROUGH CONVERSATIONS

Level 1 conversations and positive, informative and encouraging discussions with friends and colleagues can help move you forward (see Chapter 7). Why wait so long in the book before introducing you to level 2 conversations? The answer is simple – you need to have the right method at your fingertips, and the right information in your portfolio. In other words, a reasonably well-developed CV and a clear answer to the question 'what are you looking for?'

I'M STILL SUSPICIOUS ABOUT NETWORKING

Of course you are. If you weren't, you'd be out there doing it now, quite naturally, without even thinking about it. Most people looking for a job hate the *idea* of networking (see Chapter 7), but most of them will learn do it some of the time, and many will learn how to do it well, in a way that impacts the rest if their career. If you don't want to talk to strangers, then remember the advice of career coach Al Owens of Albion Insight:

> Identify the 'ultimate stranger' – your next boss. All of your job hunting efforts should then be focused on how to introduce yourself to that decision-maker.

JOB OFFER ROULETTE

When I am working with a new client I imagine we're sitting in a casino looking at a big roulette table. Each oblong on the tabletop represents one way someone might land a job. One is labelled *advertised positions*, for example, and others *direct applications*, *job boards*, *recruitment agencies*, *internships* and *word of mouth*. Where do we place our chips? Looking at the roulette table it's clear that some squares give much better odds. To some these facts are obvious, to others a mystery.

Then I ask two questions. The first is 'how are you looking for a job right now, and how is that working out for you?'. Usually this is the moment when I hear about CV problems and difficulties getting interviews. The second question is: 'Imagine it's three months down the line and you've got a job. Tell me, step by step, how you got it'. Even the most ardent non-networker will usually tell me, unprompted, that they found the job through word of mouth.

Putting your money on the word of mouth roulette option isn't guaranteed to work every time. People still find jobs through other methods as well (well-pitched unsolicited applications can be great door-openers, and recruitment agencies can get you in front of people very quickly). However, unlike any square on a real roulette table, this one pays out most of the time.

HIDDEN WORLD

There is little research data available on exactly how people find jobs. In the age of social media, channels overlap – Twitter might lead you to a person who over coffee tells you about a job about to be advertised on her organisation's website. In most economies the rule of thumb is that on average one third of jobs are filled through word of mouth. Of course, that's an overview picture of all sectors and levels. As soon as you move above entry level jobs or look at specialised sectors, or you look at new, small organisations, the proportion of jobs filled by conversations and connections can be anything up to 80%.

In any market, no matter how transparent on the surface, a large proportion of jobs are either not advertised or already have someone's name on them before the first interview. This unadvertised market has long been described as 'hidden', and there are consultancies, websites and even apps which promise access – an absurd idea, because hidden jobs are by their nature not catalogued. Hidden jobs are filled, and found, using a different mindset. Often an employer appears to be operating openly and transparently, but behind the scenes is trying to get the right people quickly, at minimum risk. This inclines employers towards people they know something about.

It's easier to work with people who have no preconceptions about how to look for a job. They tend to have a much more direct buyer/seller approach. They instinctively look for opportunities to meet decision makers because that considerably improves their chances.

Some people express ethical objections to the idea that you might talk your way onto a shortlist, or the way young people with great social connections secure top internships. Surely all jobs need to be advertised, if not just for fairness but to guarantee a strong talent pool?

You've heard the cynical line 'It's not what you know, it's who you know'. It's a good phrase to hide behind; a good excuse not to find anyone to help. The sentence should end who you *get* to know. The process is about making an active choice to get to know more people. You're most likely to get any job through somebody you talk to in the next three months – people you already know, people you have yet to meet. Yes, some jobs are still given out by family, friends, people who went to your school or share some other tribal allegiance, but far more often the job goes to someone who is just plain visible. No matter your age, class or background, the best tool for finding things out is talking to people, and building long-term relationships with the people you meet is often the key to a satisfied career.

So is the hidden job market unfair? Yes, in the sense that in any competition some players understand the rules better than others. Applying only for advertised jobs because that's somehow 'fairer' is a great way of extending your job hunt time, and a watertight strategy for avoiding some of the most interesting opportunities on the planet. They won't be in the Help Wanted section, because right now they're brewing away in the brain of someone you might just meet, pretty soon, if you simply start asking the best career question ever: 'who else should I be talking to?'

PLANTING MESSAGES

The problem is that we don't really know how or why *word of mouth* happens, and it comes as a surprise to most people that we have a large influence over it. You know your hidden jobs strategy is working when *your name comes up for the right reasons when you're not in the room.*

Picture the scene. Two people meet at the coffee machine. One of them is someone you know. Your name comes up in conversation, perhaps because the organisation in question has a problem that needs solving. How much will your contact say about you? Your CV contains up to 200 pieces of information.

At interview you might communicate 30 or so key points. Think about the last time you recommended someone – how many pieces of information do you mention in casual conversation? In everyday conversation even if we are strongly recommending someone we tend to communicate no more than three or four pieces of information.

What kind of information comes up? When asked this, many candidates suggest that people will talk about their personality. This is possible, but in order to add value to the conversation your contact is far more likely to talk about what you *know*, what you *do well*, who you are *connected* with, and what makes you *distinctive*. The final card in a five-card hand might be that you're easy to work with, or it could be a personal 'hook' (perhaps you support the same sports team or come from the same home town). See the **Referral Checklist** below.

Referral checklist

What your contacts are likely to mention in a networking conversation	Your evidence – the key message you'd like to plant
Special **knowledge** (of systems, disciplines, sectors, etc. – or interesting know-how combinations)	
Special **skills** (or interesting skill combinations)	
Connections (people you have worked with)	
Coverage (organisations or sectors in your experience)	
Personality aspects or a personal hook (something about your working style or background that sticks in memory)	

Ideally, when your name comes up, so does a short burst of focused messages along the topics outlined above. Why on earth would these messages come up? Because you are going to plant them. You are going to make sure the right things are said when you are not in the room. You do this by:

- Talking about these key messages whenever you get the opportunity.

- Making sure this information is in the first 50 words of your CV and in your LinkedIn profile.

- Reminding people of them, using bullet points after meetings rather than sending a CV.

HOW DO YOU GET LEVEL 2 MEETINGS WITHOUT LEVEL 1 INTRODUCTIONS?

Sometimes there are people you want to reach quickly, for example a key person in a target organisation. You are not trying to position yourself for an interview, but you would like to know a lot more about what the organisation is looking for. However, you don't know anyone and you're following this book's advice and not going in cold. What do you do?

- Firstly, look again to see if you have a level 1 contact who can open a door for you. Ask if anyone knows someone who has ever worked in the organisation, even as a temp, intern or consultant.

- Look at the LinkedIn profiles of people you know, and search using the organisation name. Names of people in your network may pop up as suitable intermediaries.

- Thirdly, try to spot the names of decision makers you would like to reach. Again, use LinkedIn to see if they are connected to people you know.

- Finally, if all else fails, ring up and ask to speak to your preferred contact. To prevent your call being excluded immediately, it's often a good idea to start with a question about the job, but you might decide to be open about the fact that you are really interested in the organisation and believe you have something to offer. If you have a clear reason for your conversation that might just work.

I'D RATHER SEND AN EMAIL …

Of course you would. Just as you'd rather try to deal with things on the phone rather than ask for a face-to-face conversation. It's easier to hide behind technology than go to the effort of setting up a meeting. It even has advantages of speed. It takes less time to set up a telephone conversation, and just seconds to fire off an email. When you had to walk across the street to buy stationery you probably had a chat with real people and got to know them just a little better each time. When you can email your requirements you tend to minimise the pleasantries. Technological short-cuts sideline real world relationships.

If you're tempted to try to undertake level 2 conversations by telephone or – worse still – email, think about outcomes. You remember an email for only minutes. You might remember a telephone call for 24 hours. A face-to-face conversation, however, has a huge number of reinforcing elements (visual, auditory, tactile, social, remembered shared interests, the sheer novelty value of seeing someone new); we remember meetings for months, even years. Think about the difference between someone posting you a birthday present, and someone arriving on your doorstep with a present, a card and a smile.

If you want to be remembered, and if you want someone to pass on positive information about you, meet in person. Seeing people in their actual working environment also teaches you a huge amount about organisations, cultures and subtle things like language and culture – great preparation for job interviews. Be honest about what you want: 'I wonder if I could actually come in and see you. I find that I learn so much more by having conversations face to face.'

WHY LEVEL 2 CONVERSATIONS PUSH YOUR JOB HUNTING INTO A NEW GEAR

Face-to-face conversations with the right people move you forward, ever closer to decision makers. The key, according to coach Steve Preston, is 'being targeted and focused to find good connections and people who can open doors'. And what goes wrong with most networking campaigns? According to John Whapham it's 'not being selective enough and trying to network with too many people'.

Jo Bond writes:

> You need to think of yourself in marketing terms as you take your product/service to market. Your prospective customers need to be clear about your mission and vision – who you are and what you want to do. They also need to understand how you can be of benefit to them, i.e. how you can add value to them. If you cannot explain this in an effective, easily understandable and enthusiastic way then why should they pay you any attention?

Career coach Kate Howlett advises you to:

> Spend 70% of job search time on networking in direct proportion to the effectiveness of all the routes to market. Never ask for contacts to let you know if they hear of a job – how many of us hear of a job that often? Instead start genuine conversations to further research into the job market. People try to 'sell' themselves or feel that, once they have asked friends to look out for a job, their networking activity is then exhausted. You may also tend to qualify contacts and so reject them if you feel they aren't in a useful position, but clients of mine have got jobs via networking at Yoga classes, playing Bridge, a flat management committee

meeting and their 4-year old daughter's birthday party whilst handing out the jelly! Most jobs seem to come from left field so don't qualify – just extend invitations to people you like.

TAKING OFF YOUR CAMOUFLAGE

In today's labour market jungle, camouflage is the last thing you need. Visibility is what counts in the hidden job market. Level 2 conversations help – focused explorations which provide a huge increase in information, connections and job leads. They require you to reach out to people who can get you in front of decision makers.

Breaking into the hidden market isn't about old school tie networks, nor is it only for those who are great self-promoters. If success was about the people you already know, there would be little in level 2 conversations. This method is much easier than the textbook networking model of pitching yourself to people you don't know. Level 1 conversations are all about encouragement, support and idea building. They help you test out ideas in a safe environment. Level 2 conversations give you valuable information about sectors, organisations and jobs, and will lead you to decision makers.

So, if you skipped level 1 conversations (in Chapter 7), time to revisit it now, because these give you the very best start to conversations at the next level. If you get level 1 right you have painless introductions to level 2 people.

Who do you want to talk to at level 2? You probably want to talk to:

- people doing jobs you believe are fascinating;

- people working in sectors you want to know more about;

- people working in organisations which look like potential targets;

- people who are at the heart of great networks;

- people who will continue to provide encouragement

but could also give you professional feedback on your messages to the marketplace;

- people who can connect you directly with decision makers at level 3.

CHAPTER TEN

Plan B – steps to take if networking is tricky

THIS CHAPTER LOOKS AT:

- Strategies for sectors where networking is a weaker tool
- What is your job called in other contexts?
- Telling the story of your job
- Three-step evidence

WHEN NETWORKING ISN'T THE ANSWER

You may want to take a more direct approach to the job market, cutting out or sidelining some of the stages in this book. That may be a valid strategy prompted by the kinds of jobs you are applying for.

While it's always important to talk to people and ask for their help, there are sectors and types of work where it's less appropriate or less effective to use networking. For example, if you're trying to get into a graduate entry programme in a large organisation, you'll have to go through a defined recruitment process and it would look ridiculous trying to set up a meeting with the head of graduate recruitment. If you are chasing public or third sector jobs which are regularly advertised, or applying for your first job, or seeking an internship, all that may be required is a good CV or a well-prepared application form.

In some sectors unsolicited approaches or attempting to network your way into a job won't work unless you are seeking a role at the highest level. With many public sector jobs, for example, the only way an application is considered will be if it comes in through a recognised process. Here, making a telephone call to highlight your suitability for the role can be seen as pushy and unacceptable, although it is often possible to ring someone to find out more about the job details (see Chapter 11). Large organisations, too, including many plcs, often have prescribed recruitment methods – formal processes requiring you to submit an application form or CV to HR, or your application will be handled by a recruitment agency.

In these circumstances conversations with useful people won't directly get you onto a short list. However, two ground rules before you read on:

1   Use all steps which are likely to improve your message or shorten your job hunt.

2   Cut out steps because they are not appropriate, not because you want to avoid them.

We have acknowledged that many people are averse to networking. Some will never do it, but many will unconsciously create opportunities for conversations at levels 1, 2 and 3. The fact that you don't want to network doesn't mean that it won't work. Many job changers will say at the point of securing a job offer, 'I wish I'd started talking to people earlier'. Learning to have conversations with a wider group of people is a relatively small step, so even if you only do it in *your* way, and only do a little, it will still make a difference.

There are many reasons why level 1 and 2 conversations can help you even if you are applying for jobs which simply require you to go through a highly defined recruitment process. There are other channels to the marketplace that need to be mastered. For some kinds of jobs the most important tool is a strong CV, or a well-composed application form. Multi-strategy job hunting means working smarter, not harder, by using several job search methods simultaneously, with the greatest emphasis on whatever activity *gets you quickest into a conversation with a decision maker*. If following a rigid application form process gets you the interview, go for it.

Why you should talk to people about your career goals even if you don't intend to network your way into a job

● You will pick up insider information about jobs, sectors and organisations which will help you prepare applications and interview answers.

● You will gain confidence in talking about yourself.

● You can learn from other people's experience – e.g. if someone has applied for a job in the same organisation.

● Friends, family and colleagues may alert you to vacancies.

● Whether you intend this outcome or not, you will pick up information that will lead you towards unadvertised jobs.

It always helps to find out as much as you can about a sector before you get into a selection process, so it will never in fact be true that networking is of no help to you at all.

AVOIDING THE SEE-SAW BETWEEN NOVELTY AND GLOOM

Often people who are in the jobs market find themselves oscillating between two possible worlds. The first is the world of the big idea – a complete change of career. The second is far more familiar – doing the same kind of job you have done in the past.

What often happens is this. You toy for a while with the idea of career change, saying to yourself 'the world's my oyster', but you don't do very much about it. You might do a bit of half-hearted desk research, but you don't turn the idea into a Level 1 conversation. Since you're absolutely determined *not* to use networking, you get stuck into job search mode. Perhaps you send out a **Functional CV** (see Chapter 6), believing that what you have to do is communicate transferable skills. This draws you a blank. You apply for a few jobs that you're uncertain about, get little in return, and the job market starts to look as bleak and grim as the media suggests. You begin to see-saw helplessly between 'new and interesting' and 'duller than dull'. You're swayed by friends and family who tell you to be 'realistic' and forward you advertisements for undemanding but safe roles. Before too long you conclude that you won't be able to make a career change at all. Can you see a connection between evidence and decision? No. There isn't one (see Chapter 17 on interpreting market response).

Sometimes what seems pragmatic is, in the words of career coach Stuart McIntosh, to:

> Stick with your previous job role and sector in order to stand any chance of re-employment. Too many people aim first for the perfect job and then take any job (typically at a much lower level) and kid themselves that they can find a better job in the future which rarely happens.

KEEPING IT SIMPLE

Focus on doing what you can with the resources you have, using the channels available to you. This may require you to spend a large amount of your time applying for advertised positions, or offering yourself as a candidate for jobs handled by agencies.

Even this narrow-range activity requires considerably more time, imagination and lateral thinking than most candidates are prepared to give. You need to be able to describe past achievements rather than repeat old job descriptions. You need to be able to describe yourself well on paper – because your CV and application forms will do a great deal of the work for you. You will need to learn to talk about what you are good at without sounding so hesitant that you can't get the words out, or so arrogant you won't be believed. You will need to get your best evidence across at interview.

WHAT IS YOUR JOB CALLED?

Start with a review of your CV (see Chapter 6) and seek a mini 360-degree review from colleagues, peers and friends about what you do well. Career coach Stuart McIntosh suggests: 'decide with someone else's help where these strengths are best applied, i.e. what job are you looking for and what are the job titles which apply to these roles?' Then match your experience against other kinds of jobs, including roles which have job titles that are unfamiliar. Knowing what your next job is called, in different contexts, helps you find it. Look at the UK's biggest jobsites and research jobs that seem to be of interest, and again make a note of what they are called. Use these job title discoveries to guide your search.

Write and talk about past job titles with care. If they are vague or impenetrable – particularly true of public sector job titles – explain or unpack them in terms that make them more recognisable.

CATALOGUE AND DESCRIBE

Examine the language used to describe jobs you find interesting. If you're struggling to find the right language to describe what you do well, actual job advertisements and job descriptions can give you ideas for phrases you can use in your own CV.

Several chapters in this book outline different ways of cataloguing what you do well. Go back to your **Experience Databank** (see Chapter 6) to see how to build up an unedited scrapbook of past experiences. When people find it difficult to describe themselves, they often struggle to translate this evidence into something attention-grabbing.

To take a simple example, let's assume that your last job involved dealing with customer enquiries. The **Story of Your Job** table below shows how you can tell the story of the way your job started as words on paper and built up into a real experience.

The story of your job

Your job description stated …	**Customer sales advisor** Dealing with customer enquiries about our range of desk and table lights by telephone, email and letter.
The reality of the job was …	Handled multiple enquiries each day from existing customers, mostly telephone requests for catalogues or product queries.
The job felt like …	It felt good to deal with customers efficiently, solve their problems, and make them feel their calls were important to us.
What you actually did was …	I started to get customers talking about how they had come across our products and what they felt they were looking for.

What I added to the job when I knew what I was doing …	I started to tell people about special promotions, website links and, with some customers who sounded as if they were interested, asked if they would like a call from a member of the sales team.
The most difficult part of the job …	Learning enough about the product range to sound knowledgeable. Finding ways of building relationships on the telephone. Handling calls under time pressure.
The best day ever …	I persuaded one business owner to speak to a sales consultant and we got a £20,000 order the same day.

Building on the above step-by-step process of remembering how the job grew around you, you can present this information attractively to any organisation looking for proactive customer service. This section of your CV might look like this:

Customer Services Assistant ABC Industries September 2012 – to date

KEY TASKS AND ACHIEVEMENTS:

- Handled a wide range of telephone enquiries under time pressure.

- Discovered customer needs and matched them to our product range.

- Communicated product features and benefits, special promotions, winning customer loyalty.

- Improved team conversion rate from enquiries to sales of 28%.

- Turned a cold call business enquiry into a £20K sale.

REVAMP YOUR OFFER ON APPLICATION FORMS

Remember the essentials:

● Turn your experience into evidence, and turn your evidence into something that someone reading your application form will find interesting.

● Don't assume that people know what your job was all about – job titles give very little away. Tell the story.

● Describe achievements objectively, even if they were small ones.

● Use energised language, ideally using action verbs to begin bullet points.

● Match the language and terminology you use to the kinds of jobs you are trying to reach.

THREE-STEP EVIDENCE

If you want to make a dramatic improvement in the way you present your work experience in application forms or on a CV, try this three-step approach:

1   What was the **activity**? Don't get distracted by talking about personal qualities such as being reliable or conscientious. What were you actually doing? What's a good word to describe that activity so it sounds reasonably impressive?

   Example – you went to a client meeting when your sales manager was off sick. What were you doing? *Getting up to speed with information quickly, crisis management, managing relationships, negotiating, managing a difficult customer relationship.*

2   What **level of difficulty** did you face? Having started by

naming the skill you should now add something about the context and the nature of the challenge.

Example – you had to present an idea for change to a suspicious and potentially hostile community meeting. Outline the context and challenge which required the skill: *presented controversial ideas to a difficult audience, dealing with objections through clear explanation and project knowledge.*

3   What did you **achieve**? Add a short sentence which describes what happened as a result of your skill.

Example – you took an idea to your boss about improving website traffic. Tell the story which ends with: *The idea was implemented across the whole region contributing to a 35% increase in web sales.*

Jane Downes advises:

Have a list of the top three areas of interest to you in a future job, and ensure you have a tailored CV which is relevant to each individual area. Where job seekers can go wrong is in having a one-size-fits-all message – or an uncontrolled message. It is OK to advise a recruitment agency that these are your top three role areas of interest in a particular order. It is also OK to tell them you have tailored appropriate CVs for this. Where it gets complicated is if you have no defined plan about who you want to work for and what role/job title you are seeking. You then leave it in the hands of the gods to make these decisions. Bad move. You need to learn to be your own career manager.

CHAPTER ELEVEN

Target published vacancies

THIS CHAPTER LOOKS AT:

- Ways of interrogating job ads more effectively
- Responding effectively
- Advertisements issued by recruitment agencies
- Response strategies
- Cover letter essentials

IS THERE ANY POINT LOOKING AT JOB ADS?

Some job hunters never look further than advertised positions and so place themselves awkwardly in competition with an extensive field of candidates. The fact that job advertisements are 'candidate magnets' puts others off, who believe that there is no point in applying when your application may be missed in a large crowd.

However, while you shouldn't rely exclusively on advertised positions, you also shouldn't rule them out. A well-crafted application has a reasonably good chance of getting you shortlisted, if you take care to analyse the role. If you are shortlisted and perform well at interview the odds move distinctly in your favour. Applying for advertised positions can also help improve your visibility and gain you interesting referrals.

What does not help is random applications for jobs that are a poor match for your skills and experience. You might think that playing a simple numbers game will get you the results, but it doesn't. Yes, you have to reach out to a certain number of decision makers, but sending out hundreds (or in some cases, thousands) of poorly targeted applications will in fact have a negative effect. You will develop a market reputation for wasting people's time, throwing yourself at jobs you have little interest in, broadcasting desperation and collecting rejection messages which dampen your confidence.

Make your approach to job advertisements part of a multi-strategy approach. Sometimes the hidden job market will find you, and sometimes an employer only comes to your attention when a post is advertised, and then you play by those rules. However, at all times your focus is on unearthing employer needs. Cover all bases where relevant jobs might be advertised – specialist, national, regional and niche publications, and their online equivalents, plus job boards and job board aggregators (some useful ones are listed at johnleescareers.com/links). The best way to find them (ironically for those who focus on job ads as a great way of avoiding networking) is by asking around. This process of course also alerts your network to the kind of job you're looking for. Don't neglect organisational websites, too – sometimes jobs appear there which don't get wider coverage.

A step-by-step strategy for responding to job advertisements

1 Find out more. Your priority is to ask around to see if you can find anyone at all who knows something about the organisation. This will allow you to read

between the lines of the advertisement and get a stronger feeling for what the organisation really wants.

2 Get help analysing the job ad. This task is about decoding, which is a tough job without a code book. Ask people with insider knowledge about the organisation or sector to help you.

3 Dig deeper. Research the organisation, other roles and key people. Work out how this job makes sense in a larger context.

4 Deconstruct the job ad. See below for more detailed tips.

5 Speak to someone at the organisation – but only if it's invited or you are advised that it is appropriate.

6 Match key items on the short list – point by point, providing evidence to support your claims.

7 Run your application by someone who can road test it. You will quickly get lost in the detail of your information. Simplify wherever possible and ask others to check if your document makes sense and has impact.

8 Simplify and shorten. Look at your application form or covering letter and make them as brief and direct as the task allows. If you're instructed to write a three-page covering letter, fine, but otherwise a short one pager will be best.

9 Comply with the rules, carefully. Silly mistakes in

terms of information and timing can get you pushed out of the process for all the wrong reasons.

10 Allow a good safety margin before hitting deadlines – particularly with online applications. Software problems or server down time can sometimes mean you miss deadlines through no fault of your own.

ANALYSING JOB ADVERTISEMENTS

Anyone in the recruitment business will tell you that the biggest challenge of analysing job ads is working out exactly what the employer wants. There are many occasions when the information provided is vague (the employer isn't quite sure), contradictory (the job ad was designed by a committee) or impenetrable (containing insider language or jargon). Some job advertisements provide a detailed description of the job requirements, others are sales documents designed to attract the right candidates or send out strong messages about the employer as a brand.

Most job ads will provide some information about selection criteria (often providing more information than selectors will ever use). Consider this as the beginning, not the end, of your enquiry, and treat all information as if it is incomplete. However, do look at the order of information (high priority wants tend to appear early on), and do look at the language used. Then go on to find a detailed picture of the organisation from its website, particularly documents outlining strategy and organi-sational structure. Formal and informal reports, newsletters and brochures are also helpful. Search press releases for details of recent initiatives, launches and awards. Use LinkedIn to see the profile and background of key staff.

Next, look at the job title and its function within the organisation. Check out the organisation's website to see if there are others holding the same or similar job titles, and use LinkedIn to see if you know people who do the same job in other organisations. Be cautious when looking at published advertisements from less established employers. Career coach and author Brian McIvor advises:

> If it's in the Small Ads section check to see if it is a regular insertion; it could suggest a job with a high turnover rate – which could suggest adverse working conditions or poor salary or both. Look at the wording of the ad – is it precisely worded suggesting a job? If it is worded in very general terms suggesting 'exciting opportunity to add to your income' suspect a commission-based selling job with lots of cold calling. If the job offers 'opportunities for rewarding and challenging work – and you get to set your own goals' suspect a fly-by-night operation where your work will be poorly supported and badly rewarded.

JOB ADVERTISEMENT CHECKLIST

Read job advertisements carefully, several times. Use a highlight pen to spot clues which will shape your response:

- **Job title** – how helpful is this? Use Google to check out the same job title in other organisations.

- **Identity** – is it clear who the employer is. Is the role being handled by an agency?

- **Role** – what clues are provided about what the job is really about? What indicators are there about success factors?

- **Language** – look at the balance of strong, weak and neutral language. Get a sense of how strongly an employer feels about those characteristics it says it wants.

- **Mirror the language** – using a few key phrases from job documents can sometimes add focus to your cover letter and CV.

- **Complexity** – how difficult does the job appear to be? How is that likely to match candidate experience?

- **Status points** – what clues are provided (salary, role title, experience sought) about the preferred experience and seniority of applicants?

- **Level** – look carefully for evidence about the level of responsibility, and measure that against the size of the organisation.

- **Style** – what personality and approach does the organisation believe it wants? What would work best?

- **Wants and needs** – what are the 'must have' and 'nice to have' elements?

- **Contact point** – does the organisation actively welcome conversations with prospective candidates (see below about approaching before submitting an application)?

- **Rules of the game** – what do candidates have to do to safely move to the next stage?

- **Employer brand** and **culture** – what does the organisation choose to disclose about itself?

- **Problems** – your research may pick up obstacles to success in the role, for example the organisation is just about to appoint a new Chief Executive. These are not topics for your cover letter, but things to bear in mind if you are given a job offer.

CONTACTING ADVERTISING ORGANISATIONS

When a job advertisement is issued employers get a great many phone calls, both from individuals attempting to make an impression and from agencies offering candidates. Neither are terribly welcome. However, there are occasions when you might contact an organisation before you send in a written application:

1   **If there is something important you need to investigate.** This needs to be an important detail which is unclear. For example, there's no point ringing and asking about an employer pension scheme or travel allowances, or asking about something which is perfectly clear from the advertisement. You might, however, call to ask about features of the job which are important but not listed. It's also reasonable to ask if an employer will consider alternative qualifications or experiences which have relevance – this can sound as if you are making sure that you're not wasting someone's time by applying with the wrong background.

2   **If there is an explicit invitation to make further enquiries.** Some job advertisements give the name and number of someone who is tasked to answer telephone enquiries about the role, and this is often a senior person with a good knowledge of the organisation. You waste this call if you are effectively asking them to read the job description out to you. Get hold of the documents first, analyse them in depth and then use the call to put flesh on the bones by asking more. You can subtly bring in your own background and experience here, but don't sell yourself hard. That comes across as pushing to the front of the queue.

3   **Where you know someone in the organisation.** Again, make the focus of the call fact-finding rather than jostling for position. A good contact in the organisation can help you get beneath the skin of recruitment statements. For example, if the job appears to be all about introducing change, you can find out how serious the organisation is about that idea, and how far new initiatives are supported from the top.

JOB ADVERTISEMENTS ISSUED BY RECRUITMENT AGENCIES

In many cases advertised jobs are being handled by recruitment consultants. In this case contacting the recruiter handling the vacancy is absolutely vital – not just to help you clarify the facts, but to build a good working relationship. Once you have established yourself as a strong candidate likely to be short-listed you can ask penetrating questions about the history of the job, how it has arisen, and what the organisation hopes to see in the interview room.

QUESTIONS TO ASK

Plan your questions carefully. Good questions flag you up as a candidate who is thinking intelligently about the role. Don't ask the kind of standard questions you see on websites such as 'What are the key responsibilities of the position?', 'What is the culture of the organisation?" or 'What are the main objectives of the job?' – these are almost certainly covered in the job description, and the questions sound robotic. Find a natural way to ask questions about the background of the job, why it has arisen, and what problems the job solves. It's important that you do this in a conversational way, asking the same questions you would ask if recruiting for the post, for example:

- I'm just wondering … why is this position vacant?
- I'm curious – is this a new job?
- Give me a quick overview – how does this job relate to the organisation plans I've seen outlined on your website?
- Could you tell me a bit more about the challenges of the job?
- Most jobs expect results within the first 90 days or so. What are your thoughts on that?
- Great conversation, thank you. What are the next steps?

YOUR APPLICATION

1 'Please submit a CV'

The mistake many candidates will make at this point is to send in a standard CV which makes few connections to the job. Write a *short* cover letter drawing attention to relevant evidence. Then turn to your CV, and edit and reposition the key achievements bullet points (see Chapter 8). The request will usually be to send your CV by email but it rarely hurts, and often helps, to send a posted version as well.

2 'Please submit a CV with a covering letter'

As above, tailor your CV to the role, but this time provide a more detailed cover letter. Even if a detailed letter is required, try not to exceed two pages.

3 'Please submit a letter'

Some organisations ask for a letter outlining why you want the job, either on its own or with a CV or application form. If you get any sense that the letter is the primary tool for convincing a decision maker, that's where you put all your focus. If it's a long letter, use the same layout techniques that make a CV interesting (varied line length, plenty of white space, appropriate use of bullet points, section headings to assist clarity). Don't do what many candidates do: cramming so much text into two pages that the document is barely readable.

4 'Please complete and submit an application form'

Follow the rules carefully. Don't waste an employer's time by sending in a CV – it won't be read and it will irritate the reader. Next, think about the part of the application form that will be read most carefully. This is almost always the first or last section where you are invited to offer broad comments in support of your application. Sometimes the request is even more specific, perhaps asking you to match your experience against listed competencies. This part of the application form has the same high level impact as a CV profile.

5 'Please complete an online application'

Now the rules of the game are even more restrictive. Look at the task as a whole, spotting the level of detail required and where the big ticket information will be placed. Marshal your resources so you can cut and paste from source documents. Set up a folder with a text file for each past job and others for key topics such as learning so you have this information at your fingertips in the future.

Cover letter essentials

1   Head up the letter with your contact information using the same layout as your CV.

2   Double check the name and job title of the person you are writing to. Never leave this as general as 'Dear Sir or Madam' – ring up to find out if necessary.

3   Mention the job title and any reference number.

4   Write a short opening paragraph talking about the organisation rather than yourself.

5   Avoid starting paragraphs with 'I'. Keep the focus on the needs of the reader.

6   Use bullet points to draw the reader's attention to those parts of your CV which closely match the job.

7 If a longer letter is specifically required, write short paragraphs instead of bullet points, perhaps using paragraph headings to highlight the key factors you can deliver (and which the employer is looking for).

8 Close with a short summary statement about why the role is right for you and a clear call to action such as 'I hope to have the opportunity to discuss my application with you in person'.

CHAPTER TWELVE

Organise your social media profile

THIS CHAPTER LOOKS AT:

- Why the Internet gives you an edge no other generation enjoyed
- Smarter research techniques
- Effective strategies for the use of social media
- Cutting edge social media tips from career specialists

WHO MISSED THE QUANTUM LEAP?

If the Internet was human it wouldn't yet be old enough to vote. We have, in just a few years, seen a complete revolution in communication technology. The ability to exchange documents in seconds often raises expectations in job hunters that hiring decisions will be made more quickly. However, we still read at the same speed we did when everything arrived by post; it takes just as long to read a CV on screen. The quantity of text we absorb every day has grown enormously so most people try to read too much, too quickly, often absorbing less than half of what they read. This means that you have to communicate simply and effectively, whatever medium you adopt.

The Internet is a brilliant research tool for the job hunter (see Chapter 5). You can now discover more about an organisation, its products, services and aspirations, its history and key players, possibly even its hiring, staff development and retention strategies, in one or two hours than you could by spending a whole week in a business library.

SMARTER RESEARCHING

So, even if you only use the Internet and social media as research tools, they can boost your knowledge. However, you need to know how. Stephanie Clarke is a highly experienced researcher working for Career Management Consultants Ltd. Her advice:

> You get at specialised data by hearing about short cuts from people who really understand a topic or sector. Next, ask for help at your local library – many are now linked in to larger information services. If you're trying to find out about organisations, ask if your library can get you access to OneSource, Mint, Kompass or FAME. You can often get access to far better information than you will using your own resources.

Preparing for interview means starting with the organisation's website, but use LinkedIn to find out something about the people interviewing you. Search organisation names to spot LinkedIn contacts who can give you background information.

ONE STEP VISIBILITY

The real power of social media is that it opens up new worlds of connection and visibility. This is not just in virtual reality – think how many times you have heard someone talk about something they have just read on Twitter or on Facebook.

'What's the best way for candidates to use social media?' asks Jane Downes.

> LinkedIn! Use your profile to its 100% capacity, obtaining recommendations, ensuring you have a professional photograph up there, perhaps even a video profile, and summarising clearly what you have done and what your key skills are. Least effective way? Having a profile up on LinkedIn that is inconsistent with what you are actually now looking for. Consistency of signal is vital.

Career coach Julian Childs warns of the dangers of 'confusing hours spent online with productivity'. For him, the best way of using social media is as 'an extension of human interaction, not a replacement for it.'

The problem, as with research, is that most people are not quite sure how to use LinkedIn, Twitter or Facebook to assist with career change – and less sure *why*. Rather than emailing updates and news to all your contacts, send one clear message about what you are up to and then selectively send out information people will find useful, such as tips or links.

Careers specialist Keith Busfield believes that:

> People don't get the multi-dimensional nature of social media. Yes, LinkedIn is an address book and a contacts record. It will also allow you to be visible to the marketplace, but people don't know how to go beyond that. Setting out your stall is only the beginning – you've got to make sure that people are going to walk by your stall and buy things.

You will attract people to your LinkedIn page through the content on it, the groups you are part of, and the connections you make. Busfield adds:

> Too many people use social media passively. Active use of social media is about broadcasting and getting noticed. Search people out rather than waiting for them to come to you. Contribute to discussions, answer questions, become

known as an expert. Just getting onto LinkedIn is chapter 1
out of 10 chapters.

Matthias Feist, Head of Careers & Business Relations at
Regent's College London, writes:

> Social networks offer fantastic platforms for the introvert
> job seeker. If you feel insecure about going to a networking
> event, build your network by using Twitter, LinkedIn and
> Facebook. Twitter is best for this, as it enables you to follow
> others easily, and by mentioning them, retweeting them
> and linking to relevant content (your blog maybe), you can
> make acquaintances easily without having to overcome the
> barrier of just chatting to someone in an open forum. But
> as the offline world still rules the online world, you should
> use every opportunity to meet your online contacts in real
> life. It will be much easier though if you already have built a
> relationship online.

It might help to look at parallels between what we do online
and more traditional offline activities such as those listed in the
tables below. References are made to LinkedIn but also apply
to Facebook used in business mode.

SOCIAL MEDIA ACTIVITY	OFFLINE HUMAN BEHAVIOUR EQUIVALENT
Setting up a LinkedIn account	Like buying good quality business clothes and a smart briefcase. You start to look the part, and people notice you.
Using your actual name on LinkedIn	Makes you sound approachable, like wearing a name badge at an event.
Writing a LinkedIn Profile	Like giving people ready access at a moment's notice to a short, focused version of your CV.
LinkedIn headlines	The equivalent of the three to four things you hope that your best contacts will say about you when recommending your services.

SOCIAL MEDIA ACTIVITY	OFFLINE HUMAN BEHAVIOUR EQUIVALENT
LinkedIn skills list or key words	An opportunity for you to appear several times under different categories in someone's filing system.
Well-chosen recommendations from colleagues and customers	Like a stack of glowing references.
Organisations and projects mentioned in your work history on LinkedIn	Like a portfolio full of well-known organisation names and logos.
Using social media to research organisations	Like having a team of dedicated business researchers available at a few seconds' notice.
Using social media to find people	Having the best private detective service in history on speed dial.
Following others on Twitter	Like ringing someone you know every day and asking what they are up to.
Being followed on Twitter	Rather like a steady stream of enquirers wondering what you're thinking today.
Tweeting	Like popping up simultaneously at events and conferences all over the world, sharing things that interest you.
Blogging	Publishing your own newsletter, every day if you choose.
LinkedIn contacts	The most reliable, self-updating address book you have ever owned.

SOCIAL MEDIA ACTIVITY	OFFLINE HUMAN BEHAVIOUR EQUIVALENT
Building a social network	Finding people you thought you'd lost contact with, adding to your Christmas card list, finding interesting people, sharing information and ideas, learning, developing, swapping tips and ideas – like moving into the friendliest small town you've ever lived in.

And there is of course the dark side:

SOCIAL MEDIA FLAWS	OFFLINE HUMAN BEHAVIOUR EQUIVALENT
Inappropriate use of social media	Like leaving A3 photographs of your boozy night out pinned up at every street corner.
Hiding behind code words	Fine if you want to use Twitter socially or to share your opinions with the world, but trying to keep your identity vague on LinkedIn is the equivalent of sending out CVs marked 'Candidate A'.
Emailing your CV and then just waiting for a result	Like taking out the smallest possible advert and hoping you'll be overwhelmed with enquiries.
Using social media without reading other people's profiles or Tweets	Like setting out to be a celebrity chef without tasting anyone else's cooking.
Expecting your social network to do all the work for you	The equivalent of signing your name on a petition and expecting the Prime Minister to give you a call.

SOCIAL MEDIA FLAWS	OFFLINE HUMAN BEHAVIOUR EQUIVALENT
Refusing to use LinkedIn because you want to maintain your privacy	Rather like refusing to have a house number – great for avoiding post and visitors.
Refusing to use social media or email	Like locking yourself in an unmarked office hidden at the back of a building no one ever visits.

The critical factor with LinkedIn, of course, is the initial impact of your page, which is where so many candidates end up not getting the best out of this powerful tool. Good practice breaks down into three critical points:

1   Use a good quality **photograph**. This doesn't have to be a studio shot, but it needs to be competent – too many LinkedIn photographs are poor passport-type photographs. Make sure it just shows your face – the image is too small to show anything more.

2   **Headline phrases** – make these your choices, not the text that LinkedIn happens to generate from your activities. Choose a summary statement that says exactly what you do – 'Experienced risk analyst' rather than 'Mature executive seeking new position'. Your secondary headlines, sometimes known as strap lines, are generated by current positions you hold, so think carefully about whether you want your leading piece of information to be 'school governor' or 'charity fund raiser'. Your personal statement and current or recent roles form something like 80% of the overall impression of your LinkedIn page.

3   Your **summary** and **work history** are probably the only other parts which will be read in any detail. Approach this in the same way as your CV – what can you do to be

categorised in the most helpful way? What parts of your history do you want to highlight?

SOCIAL MEDIA TOP TIPS

Here's some great advice from career specialists who spend every day showing their clients how to get the best out of social media.

- **Julian Childs** warns of the dangers of gaining the wrong kind of online image: 'Don't underestimate the immediacy, reach and power of taking a public stance online, or assume that messages get read and understood the way they were intended.'

- **Kate Howlett**: 'The top three ways I recommend using LinkedIn is to keep adding new contacts from the "people you may know" list. To scroll through contacts list and start conversations and by doing a company search of "the top 10 companies they want on your CV until your retire" and then approach the closest contacts for introductions into the target companies.'

- **Stuart McIntosh**: 'Get a decent profile and photo and build up contacts to 100 plus, join relevant groups and then target individuals in your chosen sector(s).'

- **Michelle Baker**: 'Check your online career branding, Google your name … see what a recruiter will see if they check you out.'

- **Leon Hendra**: 'In my experience too many candidates make the mistake of assuming a third party will get them a job. The only person that can get you a job is you. However good your recruiter, job board or social media solution the job search still comes down to the drive and determination of the candidate. Look at the options out there and use them to facilitate your own job search, and never cede control of the process on the assumption that somebody else will take responsibility for your job search.'

● **John Whapham:** 'I have good access to people on LinkedIn. I would not ask them for a job – but might ask them to have a look at a one-page summary of skills and experience and ask them who I might contact.'

● **Jane Downes:** 'Beware of having a profile on LinkedIn that is inconsistent with what you are actually now looking for. Consistency of signal is vital.'

● **Marie Brett:** 'Social media is free marketing material, but you must be your own public relations consultant and manage your messages carefully. Although I confine my own Facebook circle to family and close friends, many clients are more widely connected. My advice to them is: review your privacy settings regularly and ensure that only "friends" are able to access your status updates and holiday snaps. I describe LinkedIn as a cross between a virtual business card wallet, keeping track of your professional connections, and an online CV, updating your contacts about what you're doing. The information about your past experience and education should be organised in much the same way as it appears in your CV; most recent experience and education listed first, a concise summary of past roles and achievements and your key skills. Give some thought to your professional headline; it doesn't need to be the same as your current job title. Let it say what you want it to say. For example, one of my clients works 30 hours a week as an administrator in local government, and is building up a design business with the aim of leaving the administrative role as soon as it takes off; her professional headline is designer and entrepreneur.'

● **Claire Coldwell:** 'The best way to use social media is in support of other activity already under way – blatant advertising is not very effective and smacks of desperation.'

CHAPTER THIRTEEN

Work with recruitment consultancies

THIS CHAPTER LOOKS AT:

- Misunderstandings about what agencies can and will do for you
- How to spot and approach consultants
- How to avoid being offered 'same old, same old' jobs
- Getting your message across securely

SOMEONE TO DO ALL THE HARD WORK FOR YOU?

Candidates are often comfortable working with agencies because it keeps them in passive mode – you hand over the problem to someone else. Agencies often reinforce this impression, suggesting that they will market you to a range of organisations. While some do, most are focused exclusively on a small number of jobs they are attempting to fill at the moment.

Recruitment agencies are an important part of a multi-strategy job hunt strategy if handled right. They range from headhunters and executive search agencies to those handling interim managers, to high street agencies handling anything from clerical staff to industrial operatives. They operate under different names but all essentially perform the same function – solving the needs of employers by providing staff, whether on a permanent or short-term basis. Their consultants have better access to decision makers than candidates, and rather more leverage in terms of persuading an organisation to fix interview dates or to make a final hiring decision.

Candidates who make the mistake of believing that recruitment agencies are acting for them fundamentally misunderstand the nature of the game. Career coach and former recruiter Zena Everett reminds us that:

> Agencies earn their living by coming up with the most
> talented candidates for their clients. They don't want to be
> in a situation where they are sending in the same CV as their
> competitors: they earn their supplier credentials by getting to
> the best candidates first and ideally exclusively.

An agency that regularly handles roles you fit will always show strong interest. What agencies find it harder to do is to match candidates to a wide range of roles. Many agencies are highly sector specific.

FINDING THE RIGHT RECRUITMENT AGENCIES

Every day agencies receive unsolicited phone calls or CVs from candidates they will never be able to place. It's difficult to spot relevant agencies from websites and listings, often because agencies claim to handle many categories of staff – this catch-all language is designed to attract vacancies from employers rather than candidates, but can give you the impression that an agency regularly handles the kind of job you seek.

Career coach Claire Coldwell advises:

> Get to know recruitment agents and view them as a key
> part of your network of contacts. They are working in a
> high-pressured environment so you need to make it easy for

them to help you. Be responsive, be clear about what you want but also be clear about how they can help you – if they don't have credentials in supporting recruitment within your chosen market, then move on to an agency which does.

What's the best way of working with recruitment agencies? Effective job hunters usually end up making well-crafted approaches to about 20 properly matched consultancies, and have a good working relationship at any one time with about half a dozen recruiters. That sentence contains nearly everything you need to know about agencies, and reveals nearly everything that goes wrong when candidates misunderstand what external recruiters do for a living. Below-average candidates register online with anything up to 100 agencies, with almost entirely random results. Strong candidates know how to find, approach and build good working relationships with these professionals who can make a big difference to shortening the time you spend job hunting. See http://www.rec.uk.com/jobseeker for advice from the Recruitment & Employment Confederation on getting the most out of your relationship with an agency.

MAKING AN APPROACH

The best way of finding recruitment agencies is to trawl for jobs they are advertising at the moment – in any media. These vacancies give you an indication of the main sectors covered by the agency. Approached the right way, an agency won't just file your details, it will make an early decision to help you.

If you want the relationship to be short-lived and largely unfruitful you will simply email in your CV to the 'info@' email address the agency uses to keep speculative approaches under control. Since it's likely your information will be lost in a long queue of emails, that's the worst way to approach an agency. *Talk to someone.* Building relationships is what matters. Agencies have been known to put forward the most

unconventional candidates, including people without sector
experience, when they know them well.

Careers specialist Malcolm Watt writes:

> Whether approaching agencies on an advertised or
> speculative basis it's still the personal contact that's
> important. Get to know who the agent is, use your contacts
> to network to him and use him as a network contact to
> other consultants. When answering an advert use this new
> personal contact relationship to try to get more information
> about the job role to enable you to construct and send a
> tightly targeted letter and CV. Most recruiters are results-
> driven extroverts who enjoy getting results through other
> people, but they are far more likely to act as a result of a
> conversation than a document.

So take every opportunity to speak to someone – and not just
anyone who picks up the phone. You want to get to speak to
a consultant who handles the kind of job you want. If you're
unsure what that is, put some more time and effort into identifying what jobs are called in your target organisations (see
Chapter 10).

Recruiter Pauline Godley advises:

> After sending your CV for a specific role that is advertised,
> leave about 48 hours and follow up with a call asking if you
> can schedule time to talk to the recruiter to go through your
> CV. Don't be pushy but be as succinct as possible explaining
> why you feel you will be good for the role and ask for some
> more of the recruiter's time.

Career coach Michelle Baker draws on her recruitment
experience when she advises, frankly: 'ask them how many
times contacting them a week is stalking!' Jo Bond's advice
is:

> Reposition the power balance with recruiters by thinking
> what information, knowledge, contacts you have which may

be of value to them. Will you be a future corporate client of theirs in the future? – if so, make sure that they realise this.

Often you need only mention a function or job title which the agency regularly fills. This may immediately get you the name of a consultant – someone who regularly fills the right jobs. You may also pick up this information from published advertisements. Research the agency and the consultant on the Internet, and then make a phone call. Sometimes you'll be put through immediately, other times you'll have to get past a receptionist who tries to send you back to square one with 'just send in your CV'. This gatekeeper mode is designed to filter out callers who want something the agency can't deliver. Show that you're not one of these candidates by giving valid reasons why you need to speak to a consultant: start with a question about the job or a statement about why you might fit it. Use the language the agency is currently using in its advertised positions, and have a clear message about one or two kinds of job you'd like to pursue. Don't get locked into a conversation about your work history until you get to speak to someone actually handling roles and interviews.

If you're prevented from speaking to the actual consultant, ask a relatively detailed or technical question about an advertised role. The job needs to be relatively close to the kind of job that you're after, but might be one that is imperfect on the grounds of location, pay or status. The point is to ask a question that can only be answered by someone with a detailed knowledge of the vacancy and employer. This gets you two results simultaneously – you speak to the right person and you are providing evidence of where you might fit.

Remember that recruitment consultants are busy, focused people looking for the right result within a tight time frame. They can provide extraordinarily useful insights into the marketplace and give you great feedback on your market-ability and impact, but only if you fit their job range. Zena Everett advises that you:

Define how you are the 'best' candidate for the job to persuade the agency to put you forward. Be very clear on your skills and what you have to offer a potential employer: give examples of your previous achievements the agent can sell to a client. No one can charge a fee for a cheap, desperate job seeker who will do anything!

Don't get too distracted by recruiter 'rules'. Most experienced recruiters freely express strong opinions on how many pages a CV should be, use of bullet points and whether a profile is a good idea. They also have views on interview technique and whether your proposed career change sounds realistic. Take all advice seriously, but don't change your game plan every time you meet a recruitment consultant and receive conflicting advice.

When you hand over your CV to a recruiter (ideally in a face-to-face meeting), don't ask for an opinion, ask for a summary using a question like 'what does my CV say to you?' Listen carefully to the reply. If the story you hear played back makes sense, your CV is good enough. If the response is 'I haven't really worked you out yet' your CV needs more work. Zena Everett adds a warning: 'Recruiters are not your friends – so don't confide all your insecurities to them, save that for your real friends or coach.'

AVOIDING OFFERS OF REPEAT EXPERIENCE

Agencies are relatively conservative. They gain credibility by sending employers candidates with obvious, relevant experience. In a tight market they become even more conservative – putting forward safe bets, 'identikit' candidates who have done exactly the same job recently. This safety-first behaviour is frustrating for candidates working with agencies who often give feedback along the following lines:

● They keep offering me the same-old, same-old I am trying to escape.

- I get offered jobs I could do in my sleep.

- I've been offered jobs at the level I was working at five years ago.

- They don't seem to understand me or what I need.

Where the only evidence available is your CV, agencies assume you want to do similar work. A CV without a clear opening either says 'same again please' or 'next rung up the ladder'. The data you feed into the system – or the lack of it – predicts the result. Only one person can take full responsibility for the way your CV message is remembered. *You.* Therefore your CV has to have a secure handover message.

The first five lines of your CV pigeon-hole you. This can be a positive outcome if someone 'gets' you immediately, but otherwise leads to false assumptions. If you start your CV 'Qualified book-keeper' or 'Change manager' those are the roles you'll be offered. Similarly, if like most CVs your paperwork emphasises your most recent job, that's what you'll be offered again. Look at the first 40 words of the document. If someone reads no further, what jobs might come your way? Review the first page as a whole. Bearing in mind that a decision maker makes some kind of pigeon-holing decision early on page 1, what thought processes are you trying to trigger?

Is your CV the kind of document that only really works if you're handing it over in person saying 'let me tell you a couple of things before you read that …'. While the document is still mid-air you'd probably explain why, although it's an accurate history, it doesn't really explain what you're best at or what you want to do next. That handover rarely happens: most times employers will be reading your paperwork cold. Writing a good CV is all about understanding what that 'cold take' is all about. With recruitment agencies, however, you have every opportunity to explain what you're looking for. In fact, that's what they want to know.

Agencies can help you move on into a very different role, but only if you explain what you're looking for (often more than once), and if you provide answers, not puzzles. So don't waste time saying 'I'm complicated', and don't assume that sending in a CV is all the explanation you need to deliver. As soon as you get a chance to speak to a consultant (see above for strategies on how to do this), deliver a practised two to three minute pitch. In this order, talk about:

1   The skills you hope to use in your next job.

2   What your target job is called, and the kind of organisation you'd like to join.

3   Your background including any information you can provide about your breadth of experience.

If, as will happen more often than you think, an agency still sends you details of the kind of job you'd rather avoid, don't lose patience, but thank them for their interest and give a clear repeated explanation of what you are looking for.

PERSUADING AGENCIES TO HELP YOU

In addition to the above complaints, candidates often add 'When I tell them I want something different they lose interest'. Here again there is a basic misunderstanding. Although there are noble exceptions, the average recruitment agent doesn't have the time or commercial motivation to advise you on a difficult career change. However, they can help if you have a *very* clear message about what you're looking for. An agency needs to understand your career intentions in very clear, simple terms – they need to get your 'story'.

Michelle Baker writes: 'don't lose faith and apply for every job – it sends very confusing messages to recruiters and will dilute your impact when a job you are perfect for comes along. The spray and pray approach will not work.' Career coach Zena Everett also draws on extensive recruitment experience:

> Agencies' real hate is candidates who say they will or can do *anything*. They want you to have real career objectives that they can match to their clients' businesses and demands. 'I am looking for a role that does X in a company that has XXX, so please call me if you get a role like that' is far more compelling.

This is of course a good way of not using job titles to describe your work, ensuring that you don't get put in the wrong box (but recognising pretty early on in the conversation that a recruiter is going to want an answer to the question 'what does this person do?'). Then move on to talk (with real examples wherever possible) about jobs and organisations you'd like to pitch yourself at. Remember that enthusiasm is as important here as facts. Definitely don't say 'I bet you don't get many people with a mixed-up CV like mine'.

Just because employment agencies are not paid to be out there digging out opportunities for you, they can still help enormously and quickly. They can also provide useful connections. Keep records of who you've approached, ideally a printed list ready to hand wherever you are in case you receive a call on your mobile phone. Zena Everett adds:

> Manage your recruiter relationships intelligently and don't play them off against each other or apply direct to an employer if you know a third party has already introduced you. You will just burn your bridges with everyone.

Michelle Baker:

> Big pet hate for recruiters – you've applied for a job, they call you but you can't remember the role. Keep a spread sheet of all your applications and attachments with details of job, recruiter and company.

Level 3 conversations

WHAT IS A LEVEL 3 CONVERSATION?

Think of the sequence this way. Level 1 conversations are tentative explorations designed to help you create maps of what's out there and build your confidence. Level 2 conversations are with people who can actively point you at interesting organisations, people and opportunities, which is where you find your level 3 conversations – opportunities to sit down face to face with decision makers.

Research analysing the factors which shorten a job hunt points to the importance of conversations at every level, but particularly level 3. Orville Pierson's *The Unwritten Rules of The Highly Effective Job Search,* mentioned earlier, suggests that on average a job seeker needs to have 25 conversations with decision makers. This is not the same as job interviews – the decision maker may be your next door neighbour or someone you met at a conference. The difference is *you are talking to someone who is capable of making or influencing a hiring decision.*

You rarely reach these people cold. You may reach them because they already know something about you – which means they know someone who knows you. They are therefore prepared to speak to you because they can see a benefit in doing so. Some kind of information about you has already travelled ahead of you through level 2 conversations, so in a way you have already established the beginnings of a relationship. You reach them for a reason: they need to talk to someone like you because they need something.

WHY SHOULD A DECISION MAKER WANT TO SEE ME?

Level 3 conversations are opportunities to talk to decision makers. These may feel like job interviews, and may in fact be job interviews. They could also be highly speculative – for example when an organisation has a need which hasn't yet formed itself into a job-shaped object. This is where level 3 conversations come into their own.

The way the hidden job market operates is that decision makers meet potential candidates at a time when there is an unfulfilled need – or just before a problem arises. You can learn to tune in to clues in the marketplace that point to employer needs – classic ones might be unexpected new orders or growth, restructuring, mergers, product recalls, or more mundane issues like roles needing to be filled where someone has left recently (see Chapter 5). These are the factors that experienced recruitment consultants watch out for in order to pitch candidates at potential vacancies. You can pick up the same information about organisations through your desk research and through conversations. Discovering a need in a conversation is of course far more effective. You can use the opportunity to find out, there and then, which individual decision maker might welcome an approach – you've got the name of a level 3 contact.

REACHING DECISION MAKERS

This is, of course, never without difficulty. If it was, all you would need to do is buy a piece of software or an expensive mailing list and you would be able to put yourself, immediately, in front of people with hiring power. What you are trying to do of course is to reach the right person with the right problem at the right time. Some people believe it's as easy as finding out the name of senior staff using Internet research and sending out a punchy letter. This can, if used with great attention to your message, be an effective tool, but it's a weak strategy for getting yourself in front of decision makers. They are busy people with plenty of people to buffer them against distractions.

So how do you reach them? Everything in your level 1 and level 2 conversations is designed to gather information, build relationships, but also to take you ever closer to decision makers. If luck is on your side you might occasionally leap from a level 1 conversation to a meeting with a hirer. For example, if a personal friend happens to know someone who is actively looking for staff this month, you may well be short-listed by the end of the week. The danger of making leaps like that is that you can easily find yourself in front of a decision maker without knowing exactly what you are going to say about your market worth (see Chapter 3). If this happens, either get up to speed fast on interview technique or have a few more conversations before you meet this busy decision maker.

Dull as it may sound, the best way to reach people you will be having level 3 conversations with is to keep working through level 1 and level 2 discussions. As long as you keep getting better at these meetings and become increasingly focused on your target and your message, you will inevitably find that you gain introductions to decision makers. You can sometimes top up this list by making direct, speculative approaches (see Chapter 15) and you can sometimes gain introductions to the right people through LinkedIn (see Chapter 12), but the safest and surest way of getting in front of real, live decision makers is to do your level 1 and level 2 conversations well. You start to seed information and shape your market reputation. People who feel they know a bit about you are more likely to want to know more. Your name comes up in conversation, and you may be approached about a role or recommended.

During your level 2 conversations, you will also learn to ask for introductions to the right people. Keep asking the question 'who else should I be talking to?' It's powerful enough to get you in front of the right people quickly. Of course, it won't work all of the time. Sometimes people don't know anyone whose needs fit your skill set, and sometimes you haven't made your level 2 contacts feel they know you well enough to make connections for you (you'll improve – connecting with people and getting the right results is a high level skill). However, don't be frightened of asking directly for an introduction to a decision maker, particularly if you know you can pitch yourself against that organisation's needs. Record your contacts (see Chapter 2).

Career coach Zena Everett sees that too many candidates are looking for a job rather than an opportunity to create work:

> Companies are hiring people who can make them money or save them money. They may not have vacancies but will always talk to talented individuals who are clear on what they can offer a potential employer. Your approach should be along the lines of 'I have solved this problems before here, and got this outcome. I know you are facing similar issues and I would like to talk to you about how I can help.' We see individuals use this approach to start work as a contractor or consultant in their target employer. This enables them to prove themselves as suitable for a permanent position.

A STRUCTURED RESPONSE

So, the right questions to ask yourself, in order, are:

1 What organisations are right for my skills and experience?

2 How can I discover more about their actual, current problems or opportunities?

3 Who is the decision maker?

4 What's the best way to make an approach so I can get a meeting?

Question 4 requires you to balance timing, strength of relationship and good judgement about the best communication channel.

Timing is critical, so if you get any kind of indication that an organisation has a problem it wants to do something about, that's the best moment to make an approach. The need may not be a problem – sometimes an organisation has an opportunity it wants to exploit, or things are going better than expected.

The **strength of relationship** you have with the primary contact will often dictate how you move forward. If you already know the primary contact well, all you need do is pick up the phone. If you know someone vaguely or don't know them at all it will be smarter to get a level 2 contact to make an introduction. Always start with the question 'how can I make a connection?' Search using the company name on LinkedIn to see who you already know, and ask around. You may need to make connections and draw in favours quickly if the need appears urgent or the window of opportunity is closing.

So, your best and preferred **channel of communication** will always be to get a meeting through someone you already know. The great thing about this method is that no one asks 'why do you want to see me?' Your intermediaries have already done their work. Your level 2 contacts will already have explained why you are interested and said something about what you have to offer (see Chapter 12).

If you can't find someone who can make a connection for you (have you tried, really?), then you might try a relatively cold speculative letter (although if you press the right buttons this can be more effective than you might think). This tends to have more impact than an email, and is less likely to go wrong than a cold phone call where you will end up saying something like 'you don't know me, but …'.

IMPROVING YOUR VISIBILITY IN THE HIDDEN JOB MARKET

Level 3 conversations are the way the hidden job market operates. Most people think that unadvertised positions are filled on an old boy network basis, but this is rarely true. What is true is that when organisations are faced with problems or opportunities, they look around for resources close to hand. This could be the temp in the next office, or could be a consultant who did a project in the organisation last year. It's highly likely to be someone recommended, and it could be the enthusiastic person who came in for an open-ended meeting last week.

ARE YOU READY FOR LEVEL 3 CONVERSATIONS?

This is an important question. Put one in the diary too soon and you're squandering a level 3 opportunity in order to have a level 1 conversation. You'll be sitting in front of someone busy saying 'I'm still working on different versions of my CV and not sure what I am looking for'. You will be highly vulnerable to questions like 'why are you on the market right now?' and totally unprepared for 'why are you interested in working here?' In short, you're wasting someone's time.

On the other hand, it's easy to find candidates who have ready access to high-flying decision makers but don't want to bother them, or at least won't cash in those chips until everything about their job hunting message is nailed down and perfectly rehearsed. You don't need to be word perfect or crystal clear to take these meetings, just good enough.

Checklist – are you ready for level 3 conversations?

- Have you got your leaving story out of your system?

- Do you have upbeat answers dealing briefly with your redundancy/unemployment/job hunting stories?

- Can you summarise your work history and skill set in three to four minutes?

- Can you describe what you are looking for?

- Do you know enough about the target organisation?

- Can you tell strong stories of times when you have solved similar problems?

- Do you have a clear reason for wanting the conversation (you know the organisation's problems and you can show how you are part of the solution)?

- Do you have clarity about what the meeting is about and what you will be asking for?

BEING CLEAR WHAT YOU'RE ASKING FOR

Candidates come unstuck at this stage by appearing to ask for the wrong things. Let's be clear. In a level 1 conversation you are asking for advice, information and encouragement. Level 2 conversations help you identify target people and organisations. Here, at level 3, you're after an opportunity to influence a hiring decision.

The difference between this conversation and a formal job interview is that very often here, at this stage, there are no job documents. The job title has yet to be decided. So asking the wrong questions (about the exact nature of the job, terms and conditions, benefits) does you no good at all. If you ask these questions you are effectively saying 'please consider me at a later date' – when the paperwork is resolved, a formal job description is published and the job is advertised. Do you really want to delay things so that you are up against a field of candidates who can also do the job?

If you want to know the right kind of questions to ask, think the language of consultancy. Start by helping the decision maker understand the size of the problem. What needs fixing? How big is the problem? What solutions have already been tried? Then look briefly at opportunity costs: what happens if the problem isn't solved soon? What happens if the decision is postponed? In this mode you're not a candidate sitting the other side of a desk, you're a fellow professional helping someone to understand their problems better. Now's your opportunity; match yourself against the problem, not the job. Talk about what you have done in the past, how you can make a difference, quickly.

And, if it needs saying, don't leave the room without an answer to the question 'what happens next?' or 'how can we move things forward?' The answer may surprise you, of course – you might be offered an interim role, or be asked to do some consultancy work. That's always worth considering but, if you are looking for a permanent position, say so and explain why appointing you will help solve the organisation's problems. The main focus of the conversation is solving a problem or grasping an opportunity, not your need for a job.

So, ask for the right thing. If another conversation is required, try to prompt it. If you hear that there will be a recruitment process, ask for an interview. If the need is pressing and urgent, offer to help immediately and see what happens.

CHAPTER FIFTEEN

Pitch yourself to employers who aren't advertising

THIS CHAPTER LOOKS AT:

- The power of well-targeted unsolicited approaches
- How jobs can be created around the right candidates
- Pitching for openings before they become vacancies
- Speculative letters – what works, and what doesn't

THE REALLY COUNTER-INTUITIVE APPROACH TO THE MARKET

As this book has made clear, a successful job hunt relies on you using all available broadcast channels. One of these channels is making direct approaches to employing organisations. In other words, making some form of communication to an organisation which might be interested in you, but doesn't currently have anything you could describe as a defined vacancy.

Statistically, at least one in 10 jobs are filled because of a direct, unsolicited approach by candidates. Of course we're not talking about a badly photocopied CV sent out with a vague covering letter. We're certainly not talking about the thousands of CVs emailed randomly to HR departments every day by hopeful workers. Let's be clear. We are talking about well-pitched approaches to organisations that might just have a niche you can fill.

Candidates avoid this activity for a variety of reasons. Some can't see the counter-intuitive point of it. If jobs are in short supply and employers don't need to advertise vacancies in order to fill them, why would anyone waste their time making a direct approach to an employer that isn't trying to fill a job?

The short answer to this question is, *because it works*. It works for both the employer and the candidate as the table below shows:

WHY SPECULATIVE APPROACHES (SOMETIMES) WORK FOR EMPLOYING ORGANISATIONS	WHY SPECULATIVE APPROACHES (SOMETIMES) WORK FOR JOB SEEKERS
A candidate turns up at the right time.	You are matching yourself to organisations where you might really be useful, rather than to the ones who just happen to be advertising vacancies.
It saves time, money and complicated processes.	Hiring processes are sometimes simplified and shortened.
The employer knows from the outset that the candidate has an active interest in the business.	You match yourself against organisational needs rather than a job description.
It feels risky letting a useful person walk away.	You might be in a shortlist of one.

For career coach John Whapham direct approaches are:

> Probably one of the best strategies for job getting. Get there before the job is advertised! The problem is identifying prospective companies. Most companies may be looking for someone at least once a year. If that is the case, about 20% of companies on your hit list may be considering hiring staff right now. The selection process can be expensive and time consuming. Get there before they advertise!

Employers don't actively seek speculative approaches, but it's surprising how often an approach out of the blue leads to something. The lowest hit rate comes if you try to do this by email. Your communication is readily screened out along with hundreds of other irrelevant messages arriving each day. An approach by letter alone can work, but your letter has to be good – very good indeed. If your approach contains any element which is about people talking to each other, for example if you are introduced by someone and then you send a letter asking for a meeting, the response rate can be very good indeed. Kate Howlett's view is that when this approach works 'the jobs are usually great ones as they tailor the job to you – not you to the job'.

If you talk to employers about why they sometimes make an offer to someone who approaches them out of the blue, they will volunteer that it is occasionally refreshing to meet someone who has thought carefully about what they have to offer and how they can match their strengths to real businesses with real needs. Such employers often say things like 'let's get her in and see what she has to offer'. Sometimes it's a kind of market testing, sometimes they will be interested in picking your brain about past employers. If they like what they see, however, it's not at all rare for an employer to say 'we don't have a job at the moment, but we'll find you something'. The strange thing is that employers do create jobs around the right people, even if there are no vacancies, and even if the organisation officially has a hiring freeze. Even if your letter only has the effect of starting a conversation, you learn something about an actual employer's needs and get a chance to ask the question 'who else should I be talking to?'.

What candidates don't often realise is that when they get close to employers on this basis (whether by speculative approaches or through level 2 conversations) the employer is far less hidebound by a recruitment process. There almost certainly won't be a job description, or even a job title. All there is at this stage is a headache the employer wants to remove, or an opportunity that hasn't yet been exploited. You end up on a shortlist with one name on it. Not only that, you also have far more influence over job content than candidates going through formal processes where the job has been wrapped up in red tape and passed to HR to be advertised. So in a sense it's always easier for an employer to see immediately what you have to offer, and why you might be a good fit. However, you do need to show a very clear understanding of the principal needs of the organisation, and a clear message that you can hit the deck running. Keith Busfield writes: 'Today the market doesn't want potential, it wants results in six weeks.'

SPECULATIVE APPROACHES

Any job hunt programme that covers all the bases needs to include speculative approaches to organisations. Often candidates make the assumption that this means mass mailing. Some outplacement firms used to send hundreds of such letters out for each client, drowning senior contacts in paper. This 'spray and pray' approach gets your CV rejected fast. Remember, however, that most letters that arrive unannounced like that have made little attempt to match the needs of the organisation. In this respect they are junk mail. If such letters are sent by email they are even easier to ignore.

Speculative approaches don't offer a magic bullet solution. Careers specialist Claire Coldwell writes:

Speculative approaches can still work but need a high degree of common-sense applied in order to establish whether there really is a need (albeit undefined and unadvertised) within that company. The link between the CV and the company needs to be very clear e.g. a recent contract which might require particular software development experience.

There are of course employers and sectors which tend to keep a closed door as far as speculative approaches are concerned. Careers specialist Marie Brett writes:

> It isn't worth making speculative applications to public sector employers; time is better spent registering with either an organisation's own electronic vacancy notification and application system, or free-to-use portals that enable access to jobs in a variety of organisations. Application processes usually require specific evidence of how you meet the requirements of the post outlined in the person specification.

Speculative approaches – a checklist

1 Identify organisations that you're interested in.

2 Among those, identify organisations which have problems you might be able to solve, and where you could be seen as a useful asset.

3 Find out as much as you can about the organisation and its needs (see Chapter 5).

4 Dig around to see if the organisation has advertised any roles recently.

5 Spot the key decision maker(s). Use gentle enquiries to find the name of the person who needs to hear from you.

6 Work out the simplest, most direct way of making contact. If you can, get an introduction from someone you know, ideally someone who already works at the organisation.

7 If a personal connection isn't obvious, ask around – ask people who have lots of contacts. Use LinkedIn to spot people who mention the organisation in their history.

8 If steps 6 and 7 don't work, see if you have the confidence to make a telephone call asking for a conversation with the decision maker. This takes a fair amount of bravado, so don't beat yourself up if you feel it's beyond you. Better to go around a problem than tackle it so badly that you are remembered for your faltering approach, not your offer.

9 If you have exhausted all other routes, post a well-crafted speculative letter with a carefully tuned version of your CV. Don't do this by email.

10 If you hear nothing, make a phone call four days later and give a value reason why you would value a meeting.

THE LETTER

Well-constructed and punchy speculative letters to employers can work well, but before you start drafting, do ask yourself whether a letter is the right approach. Could you get a better and quicker result speaking to a real person? Written communication always works best as a follow-up to a face-to-face conversation, not as a replacement for it.

A speculative letter is very unlikely to work if you are unclear why you are applying, unsure why your experience might be of interest, or if you just don't know enough about an organisation.

Speculative letters can work very well in four scenarios:

1   When certain skills and experience are in short supply.

2   When employers are hungry to get certain kinds of talent into the organisation.

3   When a hiring need is so pressing that a recruitment process seems too long and painful.

4   When the candidate is already known to the organisation through other channels.

Be aware, however, that alongside any other channel to the marketplace, the majority of your approaches will not result in a meeting. Assuming your cover letter is good, there are still plenty of reasons why it won't work. Some organisations have a policy of ignoring all speculative letters because any new hire has to come through HR. These organisations will often only consider application forms, and only when specific posts are advertised. In this case you are best (a) applying for specific positions following the organisation's rules or (b) networking your way to a face-to-face conversation.

However, the primary reasons a well-pitched speculative letter might not work are obvious. An organisation doesn't need you at the moment. Or, if it does, you haven't pitched to the right person. Or, finally, if you've approached the right person potentially, you haven't made it clear why you are worth interviewing.

The main point of a letter is to address an employer problem, not simply to announce your availability. Career coach Ruth Winden writes:

> Identifying employers that are an excellent fit for one's professional expertise is a key job search strategy. Research

the company's top challenges. Can you solve their problems? Can you make them money? Can you save them money? What do you offer that will make a real (bottom-line) difference to them? How are you connected to the company's employees and who can help you make contact at senior level? Approaching employers with that much understanding of a company and clarity about what you can contribute has nothing to do with sending off 'speculative applications'. It is a well-researched, solution-focused proposition, aimed at creating a win/win for both parties. Maybe there is no opening at present, but your approach has made the decision makers realise what they are missing and they take action as a result of your meeting. Or maybe they don't. In which case you will have made a strong introduction, broadened your networks and positioned yourself for future job opportunities.

LETTER CONSTRUCTION

Your letter was not invited, so a long document won't be read with great patience. It's going to be read by a busy person, so don't expect to gain anything more than a minute's attention. Adopt a style similar to a covering letter, but even briefer. Try a three paragraph approach:

1   Say something briefly about the organisation, then why it matches your skill set and experience.

2   Refer to your attached (tailored CV), and set out three or four bullet points summarising key pieces of information you believe are relevant.

3   Sign off quickly, asking for a meeting.

Classic problems with speculative letters

Decision makers and business owners receive written speculative approaches from candidates every week. This is how they typically respond:

- They are all about the candidate, not about the organisation.

- They are standard letters not tailored to a specific context.

- They fail to mention why the candidate is interested in the organisation.

- They are sent to the wrong person.

- They contain factual or tone errors which show a lack of basic understanding of what the organisation is about.

- They begin with a long, rambling introduction unrelated to the needs of the organisation.

- They write about an ideal or target job not relevant to this particular employer.

- They offer a message which is vague, over-ambitious or plain desperate.

- The cover letter oversells, giving no reason for the reader to look at the CV.

- Letters make claims that are not supported by CVs.

- The letter or the accompanying CV is badly laid out and difficult to read.

- The approach comes in by email, making it either spam or 'pending'. Either category means that the letter will probably never be read.

Job interviews

JOB INTERVIEWS – THE ULTIMATE LEVEL 3 CONVERSATION

A job interview is of course the best discussion to have with a decision maker. Once an organisation is in interview mode they become serious that their problem is job-shaped. They start to commit to a process and a decision.

In a sense, of course, any market-facing conversation, even a level 1 meeting, is a kind of job interview. People remember you for what you are and *how* you are, and will retain that information for some time. However when an organisation moves into job-filling mode it adopts a different mindset. Now you have to play far more by organisational rules.

You should be very clear when any conversation you're having with a decision maker switches into interview mode.

You could of course be talking to someone in a social setting and a question like 'how long have you worked in that sector?' or 'how did you handle that?' comes up. Partial interviews happen all the time, sometimes when we least expect them. However, when an organisation moves into something closer to formal job interviewing mode, you get serious clues including: a defined need, job documentation, selection events, structured questions and a decision-making process.

FOCUSING ON WHAT MATTERS

This book isn't primarily about job interviews, for that you can read *The Interview Expert*. However, if you are following the structured approach suggested by this book you will need to be prepared for key areas that can come up in any interview. These are outlined below in the following four broad categories:

1   Self-control.

2   Employer shopping list.

3   Expectations.

4   Delivery.

Self-control

A great deal of interview preparation is about making sure you don't shoot yourself in the foot. If you've got an interview, you're probably at least half way to getting the job – make sure you don't talk yourself out of the process.

The first and probably most important element in self-control is making sure that someone instinctively says 'yes' as soon as you walk in the room. The first 30 seconds of the interview have almost nothing to do with content – after all, you're probably still engaged in small talk. However, this is where an interviewer nearly always makes an initial Y/N decision based on how far you look the part. So dress, act and sound as if you're already doing the job. Get feedback from people who can tell you the truth about what you wear, and then more feedback about how you sound. Speak clearly and confidently as you enter the room, even if you're just discussing the traffic. Sit completely still, look straight ahead and await the first question. Do everything you can to make sure the interviewer feels you are easy to work with and quietly confident, and someone who pays attention to every detail.

Employer shopping list

It should come as no surprise to learn that you should anticipate interview questions by examining the advertisement and job description with great care. Sound preparation means drawing up a list of the employer's requirements and matching them point by point against your best evidence. In fact, the average candidate doesn't handle this task very well, so simply being thorough in guessing interview questions can take you a long way forward. Stronger candidates know they need to do more, and take a different approach. They know they need to work out the difference between the employer's long list of requirements and a much shorter shopping list of the things that really matter.

Information sent to candidates is often incomplete and sometimes out of date. What's more, although it may make some distinction between what is essential and what is desirable, you will never see documents that say 'now here's the shortlist of things that REALLY count'. However, when a busy manager is preparing for a job interview, that's probably all they have time to review. The average interview covers only 20 topics or so in any depth – effectively only a sampling of the material in your CV. The decision is made around a much smaller list – a handful of factors that the interviewer can and will keep in focus. Some of these topics may surprise you and find you unprepared, because they have either not been flagged up at all, or seem to be marginal to the job.

Employers rarely acknowledge that interview decisions are largely made around these half dozen issues. These deal breakers may only be touched upon in documentation, but they matter. Moving towards a job offer means learning how to interrogate the clues you're given and read between the lines. What problems does the job solve? What do success and failure look like in the role?

You have more chance of finding out this critical information by asking people outside the process. In fact, if you ask someone with insider knowledge 'what are they really looking for?' these are the factors you'll hear about, not the extensive detail of a job description. Talk to former employees or anyone who knows something about the organisation. What kind of people shine in the workforce? What is the employer most worried about in terms of hiring the wrong person? You will often find it useful to check out informally what kind of person did the job beforehand – sometimes employers hire the opposite to what they've just had.

Recruitment consultancies and people with good sector knowledge can help you in this important task of decoding. Don't take anything at face value. If an employer claims to be recruiting against 30 competencies, they won't be – somewhere in the interviewer's mind will be that half dozen things that really matter. Ask, probe, decode – do everything you can to find out the real wish list, the one you're being scored against from the moment you walk in the room, and don't leave it until you have delivered a matching half dozen pieces of evidence that tick every box.

Expectations

Look long and hard at your CV, cover letter or what someone might have said about you in a networking conversation which caused you to be shortlisted. What is the decision maker expecting to see when you walk in the room? Your task is either to confirm or flatten these expectations. If you feel that someone is pretty sure you're a good match for the job, make sure that impression is confirmed and you cover any snags or gaps neatly (see Delivery below). Give examples you haven't already provided in your CV to keep the interviewer's attention.

If your informed judgement is that an employer sees a distinct question mark against your name, or someone who probably won't be going home with an offer – then your job is to reverse that expectation. This is about interview behaviour and demeanour as much as evidence – looking slightly more calm, confident and 'together' than expected can quickly shift someone from 'probably doesn't have the experience' to 'this person will grow into the job quickly'.

Delivery

The only remaining interview essentials (assuming you are reading these tips last minute rather than doing a proper job of anticipating questions) is to make sure that you deliver in the room. That doesn't mean 'faking it' in the style of candidates on *The Apprentice*, but means being the best version of yourself you can muster on the day.

Thinking about the small number of topics that really matter to the decision maker, make sure that you provide clear evidence of achievement. You will already have done this in a CV, but in the interview room you need to make this evidence come alive with active story-telling. The only way to get this right is through careful rehearsal.

Learn to pitch each story so that it is short enough to be remembered, but long enough to be worth hearing. This will often mean a clear explanation of the problems you faced, what *you* personally did and the outcomes. Prepare to answer questions about what you learned from the experience, and what has challenged you. Don't neglect to prepare answers about your strengths (matching them against the top five requirements of the job) and don't talk about weaknesses that matter (if in doubt talk about things you can do pretty well but need to improve).

Perhaps the biggest point about delivery is the shape of the evidence you present. Interviewers respond well to engaging narratives, but they also want to understand the big picture, too – how your career has come together as a whole, how you have grown and developed. You should go home leaving the interviewer with a clear sense of one coherent story which has led, step by step up to the present moment, and the job on offer is the next most obvious stage in your journey. Sophie Rowan, author of *Brilliant Career Coach*, is a strong advocate of the idea that when you go into an interview you need a coherent and compelling story about who you are, what you have to offer, where you see yourself in the future and, most importantly, 'how that story fits the organisation and the role in the here and now'. For Rowan this is your all-important 'career purpose'. Her advice is 'choose your next career stage rather than your next job'.

USER LANGUAGE

Making your answers stick isn't just about addressing the items on the employer wish list. You've got to pitch your evidence in the right language – particularly evidence of achievement.

Dig around on the employer's website, looking at details of jobs and projects. Translate your experience into language that the employer will recognise and find energising. Anticipate problems where your work history or qualifications don't seem to match, with clear explanations, perhaps beginning 'I expect you're worried about ...'.

QUESTIONS ABOUT YOUR JOB HUNTING

As this book is focused on the job hunt, it's important to

prepare you for questions about job hunting that might come up during the interview. These might include:

- Why are you on the market right now?
- You've been out of work for six months now. How do you feel about that?
- How's the job hunt been going?

Talking about your job hunt is one area which can feel like a minefield for candidates, and needs careful preparation. It's all too easy to over-disclose in a number of areas – feeling low about job hunting or rejection letters, giving the impression that you are slightly desperate, or giving away too much about organisations in your sights at the moment. Many candidates worry about this kind of question (and see Chapter 3 on ways this topic can trip you up early on if you're unprepared), but in practice all it takes is a short upbeat response (try 'I've met some really interesting people') and the interviewer is ready to move on to ask questions more closely related to the job.

If you're doing well you may get buying signals which come across as questions about the competition:

- Which organisations are you talking to?
- Are you anticipating offers from anybody else?

For these two questions you only need one kind of answer: 'I'm talking to a number of interesting organisations but the job that interests me most is this one.'

WHAT A GREAT JOB HUNT LOOKS LIKE TO A DECISION MAKER

You could say the only way of judging someone's job hunting performance is how long it takes to get a job. Another is to say how long it takes you to get a job that is fairly well matched to what you're looking for, which is the focus of this book.

You might also want to take into account the perspective of decision makers – employers and key intermediaries including recruitment agencies. Why does the style and substance of your job search matter to them? Firstly, on a practical level, what you do enables these people to spot you. Secondly, the *way* you conduct your job hunt has a knock-on effect on your market reputation. *The way you look for a job is taken as a strong indication of how you will perform in a job.*

This is the kind of feedback managers and HR specialists give about candidates who find an appropriate and effective job hunting style:

- Candidates who don't waste decision makers' time by asking obvious questions.

- Candidates who appreciate that decision makers have very little time available.

- Candidates whose name comes up from more than one source.

- Candidates who communicate the bare bones of what they offer in the first half page of their CV or in a brief covering letter.

- Candidates who don't over-communicate – they say enough to show why they are interested, and why they might be useful.

- Messages that don't over-sell and don't make unlikely claims.

- Descriptions of skills and experience that are punchy and connected to facts rather than full of over-blown adjectives.

- Candidates whose focus is less on themselves and more on the organisation and the job.

- Candidates who are capable of describing their own

behaviours, working style and strengths without over-egging or false modesty.

- Candidates who have a visible online presence which backs up the claims made during job hunt conversations.

MAJOR ON MOTIVATION

Ask a roomful of employers what they are really looking for in top performers, and they will only make passing reference to skills and knowledge, and they will probably say very little about qualifications. They will always talk about attitude and motivation. Leave the interviewer in no doubt of your commitment to throw yourself into the job, but make that motivation sound realistic and informed so it doesn't sound like 'just show me the job and I'll show you I'm a star'. Make sure your enthusiasm is focused on the challenge at hand, by linking what you say to the job. So saying 'I'm really excited to see that you do …' and 'I would really enjoy the opportunity to …' carries far more weight than the empty 'I'm an enthusiastic person'.

When you reveal the homework you've done, show real interest – in the organisation, the issues it is facing, the people in the room. Careers specialist Robin Rose advises:

> Over-enthusiasm goes against you, but you need to sound keen and interested. Don't say you have never done something before, say 'great, I have always wanted the chance to …'.

YOUR QUESTIONS AT THE CLOSE OF THE INTERVIEW

One simple rule applies here. Deal with doubts outside the interview room. Ask smart questions which reveal your interest, not questions which suggest a lack of commitment to the job.

Even if you're uncertain, don't make the mistake of believing that an interview is an honest exchange of views about whether the job suits you. Show you can do the job, show you want the job. Leave the rest until you have a job offer in your possession.

Career coach John Whapham writes:

> I find that organisations tend to put too much emphasis on traditional CVs which are bad at communicating enthusiasm and the ability to work within an organisation's culture. These qualities are fundamental and, I believe, their neglect contributes towards the high failure rate. Following a job offer, I encourage job seekers to spend at least one day with the team they will be working with to so they can judge company culture and the ambiance of the working environment. This could further help to reduce the failure rate.

CHAPTER SEVENTEEN

Rejection, feedback and bouncing forward

THIS CHAPTER LOOKS AT:

● Planning for 'no'

● Interpreting what rejection really means

● Keeping your spirits up in the long game

● Playing a game of compartments

TOUGH MARKET BLUES

Even in an upbeat market, job hunters will hear the word 'no' far more often than they hear 'yes'. Your original question may be 'Can I ask your advice?', 'Can I have five minutes of your time?', 'May I talk to you about what your organisation is doing', or 'Please consider my CV for your advertised position'. Every 'no' has an impact.

Candidates who are struggling to make an impression in a tough job market have often heard 'no' plenty of times. If that sounds familiar, then three important reality check rules apply:

1 Don't take 'no' personally.

2 Don't fish for 'no'.

3 Learn what 'no' means.

Don't take 'no' personally

Anyone who has ever sold anything for a living knows that you are going to hear 'no' (or at least 'not yet') several times before you get a 'yes'. In fact, rejection and refusal are necessary stages in the process. However, hearing 'I'm too busy to talk to you' when you are promoting a product or service is one thing. When it's about you, it's much harder to hear. It's interesting how often people start to unravel the whole of their job hunting strategy, trash their CV and start talking about pitching for less interesting jobs on the strength of one or two rejections. Sometimes they will do so simply because a decision maker is too busy to return their call, or because a recruitment consultant doesn't get back in touch.

Often the most difficult 'no' is complete silence. You don't hear anything at all. It's easy to read anything you want into that vacuum. Or you get vague feedback as discussed below. It's very easy to attempt to interpret this so-called feedback as information. It isn't hard data, it isn't even evidence, it's just white noise.

You need to get used to the idea that statistically in the job hunt game you are going to hear 'no' many times. Most of the time it isn't about you. If it really is about you, it will be detailed, focused and you will hear it from more than one source.

Don't fish for 'no'

Some candidates play an interesting game which we might call 'fishing for no'. For example, they apply for jobs for which they are poorly suited. They send in half-hearted job applications for jobs they don't want. They apply for dull jobs they could do in a coma and tell their friends that they are applying 'just for practice'. Then they feel aggrieved that they aren't called for interview and, if they are, because they haven't been offered the job. Going to a live interview 'for practice' is like taking a driving test knowing you are not ready – getting the bad news is going to have some kind of effect. It may be something you can brush off quickly, or may impact on your performance for days or weeks. But it will have an impact, because you are setting yourself up to fail.

Stretch yourself so that you reach for jobs that are just – only just – within your grasp. Not a job you could do in your sleep, but something you will be able to master after effort. Finding that kind of job requires practice, good feedback and plenty of hard work. So it's no wonder that some candidates want to settle for something easier. Applying passively and ineffectively for jobs you can't get excited about is high risk in terms of extending your job search time, but feels lower risk in terms of putting yourself out there.

Create opportunities to test out and improve your interview techniques – don't use live interviews for this purpose. Ask one or two people who are experienced and thoughtful interviewers to interview you. This could be a general interview against your CV or a dummy interview for a real job.

Do this with someone who can give you tough but completely honest feedback on your language, tone, content and non-verbal behaviour – don't play the dangerous game of using the job market as your training ground. The feedback you get will be bland or arbitrary, and when you second guess your own performance you will jump at shadows, fix things that don't need fixing, and miss the main things that are wrong with your interview performance.

Learn what 'no' means

A rejection letter will usually say something bland such as 'other candidates matched our selection criteria more closely'. Whether you get silence or a 'no' in the selection process can mean a large number of things, including:

- The job went to the internal candidate who was informally promised it 12 months ago.

- We decided not to fill the post.

- We converted the job into a consultancy project.

- We picked someone we already know.

- We changed our minds about what we were looking for.

- We introduced new selection criteria which we hadn't published.

- We picked candidates who matched our unwritten wish list.

- We were so overwhelmed with candidates we only saw people who have done this exact job.

- We couldn't see the right evidence in your application.

- We saw the evidence but you didn't sell it to us in the right language.

- You didn't have what it takes.

Your problem is that you have no real idea which of the above variations of 'no' apply. When you don't know, it's very easy to assume and act as if the last item, *You didn't have what it takes,* is the one and only reality.

Career coach Michelle Baker asks:

> Are you applying for roles that you aren't suitable for? If you are a 70% fit or better, then apply, if it's less but you are eager for the role, then phone and discuss or send an email explaining why. Lay out clearly how your experience matches the skills outlined – what you have to offer, rather than what you want. Then let them know why you should be considered above someone with a 100% fit.

Careers specialist Cheryl Roshak adds:

> Always keep in mind that many apply but only one will be chosen. If not chosen that does not mean you are a failure or not good at what you do. It means you were not the right

person at the right time for that company. Get over it, it wasn't meant to be, and move on. The more interviews you can have targeted to your goals, the better the chance you will find the right company that will hire you.

FEEDBACK

Rob Nathan of CCS asserts that 'it's best to take a proactive approach to seeking feedback. Ask the right questions, not 'why did you reject me?' John Whapham adds: 'Requesting feedback shows employers that a candidate has a mind open to criticism and change'.

Anything that sounds like a challenge to the hiring decision will always hit a blank wall. Get feedback from practice interviews, from recruitment consultants, from a career coach. If you do ask for feedback from a selection process, don't expect too much. So don't ask 'what did I do wrong?' because that's not only a cry for sympathy but a mild challenge. A much better approach is to make positive statements reinforcing the fact that you are not questioning the result, then seek feedback in a structured way: 'I'm delighted you found the right candidate. I have to say that I really found the interview interesting. I'm sure you'll agree that we can all keep improving in terms of interview performance. I'm wondering if you can give me any pointers on what I did well, and what I can improve in the future?'

Kate Howlett's view is that:

> Feedback after job interviews is rarely true as companies are usually too nervous of starting an argument if they are candid. Sometimes however it's interesting for candidates to hear the difference between what they thought they said and what the employer actually heard.

KEEPING YOUR SPIRITS UP IN THE LONG GAME

What is the best way of remaining positive in a long job hunt?
That's an important question at a time when more people are
chasing each job. Even with the best job hunting strategy in the
world it may take time to track down the right opportunities.
Keeping your morale up and maintaining an upbeat tone in
conversations helps keep you on track.

Career coach Jane Downes is a fan of:

> Taking control of your self-esteem. This involves managing
> negative conversations you are having with yourself,
> upskilling to improve self-esteem and confidence, and coming
> up for air to celebrate milestones along the way.

Executive recruiter Cathy Kay believes:

> Job search gets you thinking about what you can't do, but
> it's what we can do and what we can learn to do that is of
> interest to the markets.

Career coach Simon Broomer asks:

> What's the best way of keeping your spirits up in a long job
> search? Keep fit. Running and some vigorous exercise in the
> gym are good ways to release frustration and improve self-
> esteem and positive energy.

Kate Howlett advises you to:

> Spend as much effort on having fun as you do on job search
> – that way you are more effective and then you won't stay in
> your next job too long because you're so scared of being out
> of work again.

Ruth Winden writes:

> Any job search can be emotionally draining, as it is only
> human to take rejection personally. Ask yourself – what will
> help you develop and maintain resilience? What gives you

a strong sense of your individual worth? What makes you feel an integral part of your family and community? What experiences help you put things into perspective? The answers will differ from person to person. For some people the answer lies in volunteering and making a difference to others in need; for others it might be spending time with family and friends; taking up a hobby they've always wanted to pursue; or finding solace in their faith. The secret is to find something that gives you joy and energy, and that makes life worth living. Strangely enough, finding that 'something' will not only make you more resilient, it will also make you a more desirable candidate.

Career coach Angella Clarke-Jervoise recalls the saying 'We leak the truth':

When it comes to job hunting, keeping up your spirits is so hard but vital, so that the truth you're emanating is as positive as it can be. One thing that worked for me was ensuring that I had meaningful, daily connections with others. I relocated for a job in the 90s that fell away the very day I was meant to start. I had no contacts, not a lot of money and no clue how to get a job, let alone what I actually wanted to do. As anyone in this situation knows, it's easy to feel despondent, but I found that if I achieved at least one meaningful exchange with someone every day i.e. one good connect call about an opening, a meeting or interview, a networking event, exploratory chat or coffee with a contact, this really helped. By focusing on the connections and exploring what was out there, it enabled me to come across positively when I met employers. Otherwise, I may never have made it out the door from feeling so hopeless.

THE DANGERS OF KEEPING THINGS TO YOURSELF

Research published by Gumtree.com in June 2012 suggested that many people don't like talking to anyone else about their job hunt. Over a quarter of those surveyed said they didn't feel their job hunting was anyone else's business and many said that they didn't like asking for help, or were embarrassed to say they were looking for work (see Gumtree.com/careers).

You need other people during a job search, particularly an extended one which is likely to wear you down. It's easy to find people who say 'settle for whatever you can get', but that simply means 'stop thinking, stop trying harder'. Choose people who are wise, supportive – people who help reframe your experience in positive terms. Their contribution is threefold. You maintain your confidence, you will find it easier to cope with rejection, and you will receive leads and connections. Keeping your job hunt an embarrassed secret simply adds to the time you'll spend doing it.

PLAY A GAME OF COMPARTMENTS

Julian Childs writes of the dangers of 'pursuing too few opportunities concurrently and consequently being broken hearted by each rejection'. What candidates frequently do is focus completely on one position, particularly if it's an exciting job or one where they are close to a job offer. This rests far too much attention on one opportunity, putting others on hold.

Keep each opportunity in its own watertight compartment, independent of others. So, if you're going for a job, go for it completely. However, make sure you also put energy into another compartment where you assume you won't get job number one. And in a third compartment assume that nothing currently in your sights is going to work out, so simultaneously you keep developing your longer-term plan. This is all about feeding the pipeline, knowing that sometimes it takes several conversations to get close to a decision maker. Even if something looks like a safe bet, keep putting energy into plans B, C, D …

This strategy is the best possible antidote to hearing 'no'. This way, when you get a job offer, you will have other job possibilities at different stages of development, which is entirely healthy. It's also a great insurance plan if a job offer is taken off the table at the last minute.

CHAPTER EIGHTEEN

Interrogate job offers

CHECKLIST – IS IT WHAT YOU WANT?

The **Job Offer Checklist** below should be used to plan the questions you ask between receiving a job offer and formally accepting the role. Some items are things that will be answered by the organisation, but some questions are best answered by people outside the organisation who can give you an independent view.

Job offer checklist

THE OFFER

- Is the financial offer about right? Is there any upward movement possible for the right candidate?

- What are the fringe benefits?

- How will your travel and other costs be refunded?

- Is there a relocation package?

- Do you have details of the employer pension scheme?

- When is the first possible date for a salary review?

▶

- Is the start date agreed?

- Will your employer honour any previous holiday commitments you have made?

- Is the job offer subject to anything, e.g. references, or sight of certificates?

THE ROLE

- Are you clear about the main focus of the job? What will you be doing most of the time?

- Is this a new job? If so, how far are the duties clear, and how much will need to be negotiated as the job develops?

- Are there goals or targets, and are they achievable? What are the consequences if they are not achieved?

- What learning opportunities can you negotiate at the job offer stage?

- What changes to the job description would you like to negotiate at this stage?

- How much of the job is routine? How long will the role keep you interested?

- How far does the job present new challenges? Variety? How much will it stretch you?

- How is the job likely to change in the next one to two years?

- Is this a reasonably good role to add to your CV? How will you explain the decision to take this job in five years' time?

- What induction training and support is on offer? How soon before you are expected to work independently?

THE ORGANISATION

- Who will you be working for most of the time? Is this a workable relationship?

- What are your colleagues like? How long before you fit into the new team?

- Have you seen tangible evidence of organisational values and culture in action?

- Have you spent any time at all with the people you will actually be working with?

- What is the organisation's track record on staff retention?

- How long was the previous job holder in the role?

CHAPTER NINETEEN
Just the Job – first steps

Imagine getting a job that fits you. One that fills you with a sense of positive anticipation when you're packing your work bag on a Sunday night. Think what it will be like to be in that job, one that you will enjoy at least three days out of five – because that's usually enough to make a job feel worth doing. Got that picture in mind?

The tools and strategies in this book will help you get that job. They give you a structure which has helped hundreds of my clients shave weeks, if not months, off their job search time.

But remember, it is unwise to rush to market. Take your time, plan wisely, prepare properly and maximise conversations intelligently and you will get ever closer to the decision makers who can deliver the job you want.

It is these conversations that are more than likely to lead to you landing the job of your dreams. Conversations with people, face to face wherever possible, give you ideas, encouragement, feedback, connections and – ultimately – a job offer. So if you're only going to focus on one part of the material in this book, remember the importance of people power in your job search.

So, remembering that luck is a heady mix of pure chance and the things you can do to improve the odds in your favour, good luck, and good hunting.

INDEX